READ AHEAD

Reading and Life Skills Development

2

JO McENTIRE

Longman

Read Ahead 2: Reading and Life Skills Development

Copyright © 2004 by Pearson Education, Inc.
All rights reserved.
No part of this publication may be reproduced,
stored in a retrieval system, or transmitted
in any form or by any means, electronic, mechanical,
photocopying, recording, or otherwise,
without the prior permission of the publisher.

Pearson Education, 10 Bank Street, White Plains, NY 10606

Vice president, multimedia and skills: Sherry Preiss
Executive editor: Laura Le Dréan
Development editor: Stacey Hunter
Production editor: Diana P. George
Marketing manager: Joe Chapple
Senior manufacturing buyer: Edith Pullman
Photo research: Dana Klinek
Cover and text design: Ann France
Cover image: Jude Maceren/Stock Illustration Source, Inc.
Text composition: Rainbow Graphics
Text font: 11.5/13 Minion
Text art: Matthew Mellett/Wilkinson Studios, Inc.
Photo credits: **Page iii,** top to bottom: © Peter Turnley/Corbis; © Tony Arruza/Corbis;
© Royalty-Free/Corbis; **Page 28,** © Bill Stormont/Corbis; **Page 56,** © Peter
Turnley/Corbis; **Page 75,** © David Butow/Corbis SABA; **Page 81,** top (left to right):
© Bryn Colton/Assignments Photographers/Corbis; © Bettmann/Corbis; © Peter
Turnley/Corbis; bottom (left to right): © David Turnley/Corbis; ©
Bettmann/Corbis; AP/Wide World Photos; **Page 97,** © David Turnley/Corbis;
Pages 106, 119, © Tony Arruza/Corbis; **Page 113,** Courtesy of Space
Systems/LORAL and NOAA; **Page 122,** Publication of the National Oceanic &
Atmospheric Administration (NOAA), NOAA Central Library; **Page 131,** top
(left): © Robert Brenner/PhotoEdit; (right): © Royalty-Free/Corbis; bottom (left):
© Jeff Greenberg/PhotoEdit; (right): © Ariel Skelley/Corbis; **Page 176,** © Dean
Conger/Corbis; **Page 179,** AP/Wide World Photos; **Page 189,** © Royalty-
Free/Corbis; **Page 196,** © Digital Vision/Getty Images.

Library of Congress Cataloging-in-Publication Data

McEntire, Jo.
    Read ahead two / Jo McEntire.
        p. cm.
    ISBN 0-13-111784-X (alk. paper)
    1. English language--Textbooks for foreign speakers. 2. Readers.
    I. Title.

PE1128.R38 2003
428.6'4--dc22

2003058817

LONGMAN ON THE **WEB**

Longman.com offers online resources for
teachers and students. Access our Companion
Websites, our online catalog, and our local
offices around the world.

Visit us at **longman.com.**

Printed in the United States of America
3 4 5 6 7 8 9 10–VHG–08 07 06 05

Contents

Scope and Sequence

CHAPTER	READINGS	READING SKILLS	VOCABULARY SKILLS
1 The Global Village	Welcome to the Global Village (expository) The Importance of Nonverbal Communication (expository) Brown Eyes–Blue Eyes (short story)	Previewing a reading Identifying paragraph topics	Previewing vocabulary Using adjectives to describe feelings Using words from other languages
2 Safety Matters	Fire Safety 101 (expository) Fire Safety at Ashton Apartments (informational flyer) Be Safe, Not Sorry! (short story)	Previewing a reading Finding main ideas Predicting Scanning for details Recognizing a sequence of events	Using context clues to understand vocabulary Using suffixes: *-ful* and *-less*
3 Voting Counts	Are All Elections Fair? (expository) It's Time to Change! (flyer – persuasive) The Future Is Bright! (flyer – persuasive) A Question of Citizenship (expository)	Previewing a reading Finding main ideas Predicting Distinguishing facts from opinions	Previewing vocabulary Using context clues to understand vocabulary Understanding and using the suffix *-tion*
4 Leaders of Yesterday	King Hussein of Jordan (expository – chronological) Indira Gandhi (expository – chronological) Nelson Mandela (expository – chronological)	Previewing a reading Identifying supporting details Identifying and using time phrases Distinguishing facts from opinions Recognizing time clauses Paraphrasing Highlighting	Using context clues to understand vocabulary

LIFE SKILLS	WRITING ACTIVITIES	ONLINE ACTIVITIES
Getting to know people Searching for information on the Internet	Short answers Paragraph practice	Researching other countries Preparing to visit a country or a city as a tourist
Planning an escape route Completing an accident report	Report writing Paragraph practice	Researching fire safety for children Finding basic first aid on the Web Learning how to prepare for natural disasters
Answering citizenship questions Reading and discussing election flyers	Giving reasons Paragraph practice Designing a flyer	Finding sample citizenship questions Researching statistics on the Web Discovering how to register to vote
Keeping up on current events Searching for information on the Internet	Short answers Paragraph practice Writing from notes	Researching a famous person Finding "Today in History" Researching the origin of the Nobel Peace Prize

LIFE SKILLS	WRITING ACTIVITIES	ONLINE ACTIVITIES
Understanding weather terms Searching for information on the Internet	Completing paragraph outlines Taking notes	Researching global warming Researching the causes of earthquakes or volcanic eruptions Searching online for weather reports
Understanding help wanted abbreviations Describing personal skills Résumé writing Researching interview questions online	Résumé writing Completing a résumé worksheet Writing an advertisement	Searching for different styles of résumés Finding online employment ads Researching common interview questions
Understanding a paycheck Making a personal budget Researching online	Writing a paragraph summary Paragraph practice Writing a letter to a supervisor Writing a memo	Researching to find current economic rates (i.e., mortgage rate, unemployment rate, inflation rate) Finding out the qualities that employees seek from jobs and managers want from employees Researching the topic of child labor
Understanding rating systems	Writing a review Finishing a short story	Finding movies suitable for children of different ages Finding current movie reviews

Introduction

Teachers today are faced with the challenge of meeting more divergent student goals than in the past. While life and workplace skills are critical to the success of students, employment trends indicate that students also need higher-level academic skills to succeed in job training programs and to advance in their fields. *Read Ahead 2* is informed by Equipped for the Future Standards, helping students build the skills they need to communicate with confidence, make informed decisions, work with others cooperatively, and take responsibility for their own learning.

Text Organization

Read Ahead 2 has eight chapters, each consisting of three thematically linked readings. Each chapter's opening page includes a brief description of the three readings and a preview of the reading, vocabulary, and life skills practiced in the chapter. Chapters are organized as follows:

Before You Read

Before each reading, students are asked questions to activate their knowledge about the subject of the reading. Key vocabulary is introduced to aid students' comprehension of the reading.

Now Read

Each of the three chapter readings explores a different aspect of the theme. Throughout the book, students are exposed to a variety of text types, ranging from exposition to résumés to movie reviews.

After You Read

Each reading is followed by *How Well Did You Read?* and *Check Your Understanding* questions that check students' general understanding of the reading. In addition, one or more exercises that give students practice in reading or vocabulary skills may follow. These include *Identifying Supporting Details, Distinguishing Facts from Opinions,* and *Using Context Clues to Understand Vocabulary.*

Expanding the Topic

This section, located at the end of each chapter, includes writing topics that allow students to apply the content and vocabulary they have learned (*Connecting Reading with Writing*) and asks students to find out more about the topics by completing guided online searches (*Exploring Online*).

Reading, Vocabulary, and Life Skills

Reading, vocabulary, and life skills are clearly and concisely presented in skill boxes throughout each chapter and are recycled throughout the book. Reading skills include previewing, predicting, distinguishing between fact and opinion, and identifying paragraph topics. Vocabulary skills include understanding word forms, suffixes and prefixes, guessing meaning through context, and using adjectives to describe feelings. Life skills address topics such as completing an accident report, describing personal skills, practicing job interview questions, and writing a résumé.

As students progress through this text, they will work with classmates to develop confidence in reading and communicating about their reading, learn about making informed decisions, and ultimately, take responsibility for their learning. In short, they will become more independent learners, able to make the transition to academic studies and to become lifelong learners.

Teacher's Manual

The teacher's manual includes general "teaching the chapter" guidelines, teaching suggestions for specific chapters, and Chapter Review Tests. Each test includes vocabulary items from the chapter and comprehension questions about a reading passage related to the chapter theme. The tests are designed to be given within a class period, and provide valuable feedback to students and teachers about student progress in building reading and vocabulary skills. Answer keys for the student book exercises and Chapter Review Tests are also provided.

About the Author

Jo McEntire has been an English language instructor for over twenty years. She is on the faculty of Shoreline Community College in Seattle, Washington, where she has served as Director of Adult Basic Education as well as Program Chair for English language learning. Ms. McEntire has also taught in Botswana, Africa, and Oman. She is a graduate of Manchester University in England.

Acknowledgments

I would like to thank Laura Le Dréan, Executive Editor at Longman, for her tireless support in helping me translate an idea into a text, Stacey Hunter and Jennifer Bixby for their thoughtful and intelligent editing, and Dana Klinek for her diligent work on several aspects of the project, notably on the photo research and Teacher's Manual. I would also like to acknowledge the exceptional ESL faculty and students at Shoreline Community College who provided wonderful ideas and thoughtful feedback. Finally, my thanks go to Scott, Tess, and Tom for their support, love, and laughter.

Jo McEntire

The Global Village

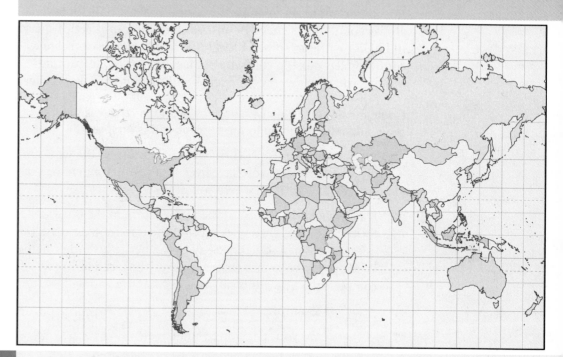

This chapter begins by helping you get to know the other students in your class and your teacher. Reading 1 explains the idea of the global village and describes international communities today. Reading 2 looks at communication between people of different cultures. Reading 3 is a short story about a truly global family.

In this chapter, you will practice:

Reading Skills
- → Previewing a reading
- → Identifying paragraph topics

Vocabulary Skills
- → Previewing vocabulary
- → Using adjectives to describe feelings
- → Using words from other languages

Life Skills
- → Getting to know people
- → Searching for information on the Internet

Welcome to the Global Village

Before You Read

It is important to get to know the people in your class for several reasons. First, it's always good to make new friends. Second, you can practice speaking and listening in English with each other. Most importantly, you learn more when you are feeling comfortable, enjoying yourself, and feeling part of a community. When you are relaxed, you won't worry so much about making mistakes and asking questions.

Complete the activities with your classmates. This will help you get to know each other and introduce you to the subject of this chapter.

1. Work in small groups. Turn back to page 1. Use the world map to show your group other places you have lived or a country where you have relatives. Explain why you live where you do now.

2. Play *Global Bingo!* Look at the information in the boxes on page 3 to help you form questions. Then walk around the classroom and ask other students the questions. When someone answers *yes,* write his or her name in that box. When you have names written in every box, call out *Bingo!* The first person to complete the boxes and call out *Bingo!* is the winner.

   Example:

   Do you speak three languages?

   Have you bought a McDonald's hamburger in more than one country?

   Do you enjoy Chinese food?

Global Bingo

_____ (name) speaks three languages.	_____ (name) drives a Japanese car.	_____ (name) has a friend who speaks a different first language.
_____ (name) has bought a McDonald's hamburger in more than one country.	_____ (name) has citizenship in two countries.	_____ (name) enjoys Chinese food.
_____ (name) uses a bilingual dictionary.	_____ (name) buys groceries in an Asian grocery store.	_____ (name) speaks English at home.
_____ (name) has a neighbor who speaks a different language.	Global Bingo!	_____ (name) celebrates the Chinese New Year.
_____ (name) has used chopsticks.	_____ (name) listens to music sung in different languages.	_____ (name) e-mails friends who live in a different country.
_____ (name) knows children who speak two languages.	_____ (name) watched American movies as a child.	_____ (name) has family living in a different country or city.
_____ (name) can name the leaders of five countries.	_____ (name) enjoys baseball.	_____ (name) plans to work in a different country or city.

Using Previewing Strategies

Before you begin to read, you need to "warm up" your mind just like people warm up before they exercise. Warming up before you read is called **previewing.** Previewing is looking at certain parts of a text before you read it. It helps you understand a text quickly and clearly.

To preview,

- read the title and the headings and look at any illustrations. This will give you the topic.
- think about what you already know about the topic. Have you read about it in your first language? Have you talked about it or seen movies or television programs about it?

At first, previewing takes a little time. You will get faster as you practice and you will understand more the first time you read something.

A. Before you begin Reading 1 on pages 6 and 7, preview this book. Quickly look at the table of contents on page iii and the pages in Chapter 1. Answer the following questions as quickly as possible.

1. How many chapters are there? _____

2. What are the titles of the first four chapters? _____

    _____

3. What is the last activity in each chapter? _____

4. How are skills introduced? _____

B. Work in small groups to preview Reading 1. Answer the following questions.

1. What's happening in the illustration on page 6?

2. Do you live in a neighborhood like this?

3. What is the connection between this picture and *Global Bingo!*?

4. Now look at the title of the reading. What do you think a global village is? What is the connection between a global village and the illustration on page 6?

Previewing Vocabulary

These words are in Reading 1. Read the words and their definitions. Then choose the best word to complete each sentence.

Word	Definition
border	the official line that separates two countries
chat	communicate online in a friendly, informal manner
exports	sells or sends to another country
generation	the average period of time between birth of adults and birth of their children
go online	connect to the Internet
reflects	represents or shows
settled	began living in a place for a long time
surf	search on the Internet for different Web sites

1. You usually need a passport or a visa when you cross the _____ from one country to another.

2. My family has lived in this city for more than one _____. My great-great-grandparents moved here over a hundred years ago.

3. The teacher told the students to _____ and find more information about opportunities to study overseas.

4. I love to _____ online with my friends in Japan. It's a lot cheaper than calling by phone.

5. An ESL class often _____ the world. Students from many different countries and cultures are together in one classroom.

6. After Anna left Poland, she moved to New York for a short time before she finally _____ in San Diego. She's still living there.

7. My father is a Korean businessman, and he lives in Seoul, Korea. He _____ tea from Korea and sells it to companies in England.

8. Maria likes to _____ the Web. In fact, she spends hours looking at different Web sites every day.

Welcome to the Global Village

1   Just two generations ago, at the time our grandparents were children, the world was a much larger place. Most of our grandparents never traveled from their country of birth. Many people throughout the world never watched television regularly. Nonstop international news on stations like CNN didn't exist. There was no World Wide Web to surf; in fact, many of our parents didn't have their own telephone. International travel was difficult. Airfares were very expensive, and some countries, like China and the former Soviet Union, did not allow their citizens to go freely to other countries. Students studied in their country of birth and very rarely went overseas to learn a language or continue their education. People of that generation traveled the world only through books and their imaginations.

continued

2   Today the world feels much smaller. We can easily visit different countries as tourists, students, and workers. We settle in different countries, bringing our languages and cultures with us. We can turn on the TV, open a newspaper, or go online and instantly find out what is happening around the world. We e-mail our friends who live across seas and mountains. We eat American food in Tokyo and Japanese food in Miami. Many of us speak more than one language, and we have children whose first language is not our first language. Many countries have opened up their borders. For example, people from all over Eastern Europe now enjoy the freedom to travel. The whole world has opened up.

3   So welcome to the global village—a new world which seems smaller because we are all more closely connected. We now live in a world where ideas, goods, and people move easily across borders.

4   In the global village, one small community reflects the larger world. Businesses import and export goods from different countries. Of course, many communities have a McDonald's and a Starbucks. There is also a small Mexican restaurant two doors down from a Vietnamese restaurant. There's an Internet café where you can go online and chat with faraway friends. Across the street is a Korean mall with Korean hairdressers, grocery stores, and a health clinic. As you wait to cross the street, Japanese, European, Korean, and American cars race by. Everywhere you go, you see people who look like you and people who look different from you. You hear people talking in your language, and you hear the musical sounds of other languages. The global village is where you live. It's your neighborhood. It's your home.

After You Read

How Well Did You Read?

Work with a partner. Read the statements. Write *T* (true) or *F* (false). Underline the information in the reading that supports your answer.

_____ 1. Technology has made it easier for people to find out more about the world.

_____ 2. Our grandparents only knew about other countries by going online and searching the Web.

_____ 3. Today, more people live international lifestyles than in the past.

_____ 4. It is easier to travel today because the Earth is getting smaller.

_____ 5. More people live in diverse neighborhoods today than in the past.

Check Your Understanding

A. Discuss the questions in small groups.

1. Do you think this reading accurately describes the life of your grandparents? Why or why not?

2. In your neighborhood, are there restaurants, stores, and businesses from different areas of the world? Is it easy to buy food and other products from different countries?

3. How often do you telephone, write, or e-mail someone in a different country?

4. What do you think your grandparents would like about the global village? What would they dislike?

B. Work with a partner. Circle the letter of the best answer.

1. Our grandparents didn't usually travel out of the country because _____ .

   a. the world was bigger than it is today
   b. people did not want to travel
   c. travel was more difficult than it is today

2. According to the reading, our grandparents usually learned about other countries through _____ .

   a. reading
   b. surfing the Web
   c. studying overseas

3. *The whole world has opened up* (paragraph 2) means _____ .

   a. people from all over the world can now travel freely
   b. new businesses opened around the world
   c. it is much easier to learn about other countries

4. The global village reflects the larger world because _____ .

   a. villages around the world are much larger
   b. communities are multicultural with people from many different countries
   c. communities are small places with a lot of people

5. The following sentence tells you that the writer likes this new world:
   _____ .

   a. Today the world feels much smaller
   b. The whole world has opened up
   c. So welcome to the global village

Think About the Reading

A. Work in small groups to complete the following activities.

In *Global Bingo!,* you discovered that your classroom is like a global village. Your class may have students from many different countries who speak different languages. Or perhaps you are from the same country, but you prefer different foods and you enjoy different music. Some of you may have relatives in a different country. You are probably wearing clothes that were made in other countries. Now think about a smaller global village: your group. Complete these activities with your group members.

1. Introduce yourselves. Make sure you know each other's names.

2. Talk about how you and your group members are different from each other. Now make a list of three differences. Make sure you write down the names of the classmates you are writing about.

   Example:
   I speak Spanish at home, and Victor speaks Ukrainian. Marta speaks Polish.

   a. _____

   b. _____

   c. _____

3. Now talk to your group about how you are similar to each other. For example, do you have similar goals? Have you had similar experiences where you are living? Do you enjoy similar activities? Make a list of these similarities. Make sure you write down the names of the classmates you are writing about.

   a. _____

   b. _____

   c. _____

B. How "global" are you? Take the following quiz. Then discuss your answers with your group.

1. How many languages do you speak? _____

2. If you have a car, where was it made? _____

3. Where was your watch made? _____

4. How many countries have you visited? _____

5. What's your favorite kind of food? _____

6. Name one other country you have lived in. _____

7. Who is your favorite singer? _____

8. Why are you learning English? _____

Identifying Paragraph Topics

A **paragraph** is a group of sentences about the same subject. The subject is called the **topic.** Readers need to understand the paragraph topic in order to understand the paragraph. To identify the topic, you should ask "What's this paragraph about?" As you practice identifying the topic, remember:

- a topic is usually expressed as a word or a phrase; it is not expressed as a sentence.
- a topic should not be too specific, nor too general.

Example:

The Internet makes it easier for people to communicate. Past generations used to write letters to each other and wait for weeks to receive the reply. Today, communication is almost instant. Go online, type in the e-mail address, and send your message. It will be a matter of seconds, not weeks, before your message arrives. If you have the popular instant messaging offered by most ISPs (Internet Service Providers), you can communicate in a matter of seconds with several friends at the same time. E-mail is also a cheap way to communicate, especially if you want to chat with someone who is living in a different country. There is no doubt that the Internet makes communication easier, quicker, and cheaper.

What's this paragraph about? <u>Advantages of the Internet</u>

Read the paragraphs. Circle the letter of the best answer to each question.

1.   My Saturday mornings as a child were special. My mother used to take me shopping every Saturday. First, we would go to the fish shop to buy our fish. The next stop was the butcher's, where we would choose the meat for our Sunday dinner. Next door was the fruit and vegetable store. I loved looking at all the fresh, colorful vegetables stacked up on the tables. Sometimes the shop owner would give me an apple as a treat. Our final stop was always the bakery. I still remember the wonderful smell of freshly baked bread. Those were special days.

What's the topic?

a. Different shops
b. Saturday shopping as a child
c. Shopping for vegetables

2.   Grocery stores today are very different from stores two generations ago. Today you only need to go to one store to buy everything you need for the week. You can find meat, fish, dairy products, fruit and vegetables, and any other grocery item you are looking for—all in one store. In the past, you had to go from one shop to another for all your needs. Also, today you can find a much wider selection of food. Grocery stores also reflect our multicultural world. You can find Mexican, Chinese, and Thai food in almost every large grocery store. This was impossible in the past. Finally, stores today import fruit and vegetables from all over the world. You can buy fresh strawberries from Chile in February and tomatoes all year round. Grocery stores have changed a lot since my grandmother's time.

What's the topic?

   a. how grocery stores have changed
   b. fresh food in grocery stores
   c. grocery stores

3.   Not very long ago, a businessman named Ted Turner had an idea. He wanted to create a twenty-four-hour television news channel. At the time, a lot of people laughed at this idea. They believed people only wanted to watch the news in the evening. Turner disagreed, however, and started CNN, or Cable News Network. CNN quickly became one of the most watched channels on TV. It is still popular today, not only in the United States but around the world.

What's the topic?

   a. Ted Turner
   b. CNN
   c. how CNN began

4.   People who have never been to the United States sometimes have an inaccurate idea about life in America. They watch Hollywood movies full of beautiful, rich people and think that everyone in the States is like this. They see violent American TV programs and think that life in the United States is very dangerous. They visit McDonald's in their own country and think that all Americans eat hamburgers every day. When people visit America, however, they find that life is very different from what they see in movies and on TV.

What's the topic?

   a. Hollywood movies
   b. learning about U.S. life through movies and TV
   c. visiting America

The Importance of Nonverbal Communication

Before You Read

Previewing

A. Work in small groups. Look at the illustrations. Discuss what the people are doing and how they feel. Then read situations 1 and 2 below.

Situation 1

Ali and Hiro are having a conversation. They're both uncomfortable. In Ali's culture, people usually stand close to each other. In Hiro's culture, people stand farther apart, and they don't touch.

Situation 2

Mr. and Mrs. Harrison invited Mr. and Mrs. Vargas for dinner at 7:00 p.m. It's 7:30 p.m. and the Vargases have not arrived yet. In the Harrisons' culture, people arrive for dinner on time, or just a few minutes late. In the Vargases' culture, it is polite to be at least a half hour late for a dinner invitation.

B. Now preview Reading 2 on pages 14 and 15. Read the title and look at the illustrations. What do you think nonverbal communication is? Why is it important?

Previewing Vocabulary

These words are in Reading 2. Read the words and their definitions. Then choose the best word to complete each sentence.

Word	Definition
ignore	not pay attention to something or someone
make eye contact	look straight at someone's eyes
multicultural	including people and ideas from many different countries and cultures
prefer	like one thing more than another thing
respect	polite behavior towards an important person
rude	not polite
say (no) directly	clearly refuse
silence	no noise; quiet
translator	person who changes writing or speech to a different language
uncomfortable	not relaxed; nervous

1. America is a _____ country. People from all over the world have settled here.

2. People show _____ in different ways. For example, in some Asian countries, young people do not look into the eyes of older people when speaking to them.

3. Shy people often feel _____ if they have to speak in front of the class.

4. I sometimes _____ other people's mistakes. I pretend I don't see the mistake.

5. When the Russian president talks to the Canadian prime minister, they need a _____ to make sure they understand each other.

6. A young Vietnamese man does not _____ with an older person. He lowers his eyes because this is polite in his culture.

7. Americans often feel nervous when there is _____ in a conversation. They like to continue talking.

8. Many people find it difficult to _____; they don't want to be impolite.

9. I _____ green tea to coffee. May I have some green tea, please?

10. In Western culture, it is _____ to make loud noises when you are eating. However, in some Asian cultures, making loud eating noises shows that the food is good.

The Importance of Nonverbal Communication

1   People communicate in several ways. They communicate through words (verbal communication) and body language (nonverbal communication) by using gestures and changing facial expressions. If the speaker communicates well, the listener will understand exactly what the speaker means. However, if there is a problem in communication, the listener will get the wrong message. Surprisingly, nonverbal communication often causes the most communication problems between people of different cultures.

2   Take, for example, this situation. A French sales representative, Pierre, goes to Japan to meet with Mr. Ataki and Mr. Tanaka, managers of a large company. Pierre has never been to Japan before, and he has no experience working with Japanese businesspeople. He is a good sales representative, however, and he is excited about the trip. He doesn't speak Japanese, but he will have a Japanese translator, so he is not worried about communication. When Pierre first meets Mr. Ataki and Mr. Tanaka, he steps forward to shake hands. They ignore his hand and bow. To hide his embarrassment, he laughs and slaps them on the back. They step back and smile. He sees their smiles and smiles back.

3   After they introduce themselves, Pierre begins to talk about his company. The Japanese businessmen nod their heads, and Pierre is happy they agree with him. Then there is silence, and Pierre feels uncomfortable. So he asks another question and talks a little louder. This time, Mr. Ataki replies, but as he speaks, he looks toward the ground. Pierre doesn't understand why Mr. Ataki won't look at him. Pierre thinks he might be hiding something. At the end of the meeting, the Japanese men bow again and thank Pierre for coming. They say they have enjoyed meeting with him, and they like his business ideas. Later that evening, Pierre's boss calls and asks how the meeting went. "It went very well," replies Pierre. "At least I think it did."

continued

4   In this example, Pierre thought he communicated his message, but the Japanese men received a very different message. When Mr. Ataki and Mr. Tanaka communicated their message nonverbally, Pierre received a different message. There was, in fact, very little communication going on. A week later, Pierre heard that his trip was unsuccessful. The Japanese company chose a different company to work with.

5   What did Pierre do wrong? His words were polite, and the translator translated them correctly. His verbal communication was not the problem. However, his nonverbal communication was confusing and rude to the Japanese businessmen. In addition, Pierre did not understand their nonverbal messages. Here are some of Pierre's mistakes:

- Pierre tried to shake hands. Japanese people usually prefer to bow in formal business situations.
- Pierre was embarrassed, so he slapped the men on the back. Japanese people dislike being touched in public.
- When he saw the men smile, he thought they liked his behavior. In fact, they were smiling because they were embarrassed by his rudeness.
- When Pierre saw the men nod, he thought they agreed. They were actually just showing that they were listening.
- When the men didn't reply quickly, Pierre felt uncomfortable and talked again. He didn't realize that silence is an important part of communication in Eastern cultures. The Japanese men were showing respect by thinking seriously about his words.
- One of the men showed respect again by not making eye contact; Pierre thought he was hiding something.
- At the end of the meeting, Pierre thought the men agreed with his proposal. He heard them say *yes*. He did not understand that to say *no* directly is rude in Japan. An indirect *yes* can mean *no*.

6   In this business meeting, the nonverbal communication was misunderstood. As Pierre found out, nonverbal communication between people of different cultures can be very confusing. To communicate well in a multicultural world, people need to understand both verbal and nonverbal communication styles. As Pierre discovered, if you are meeting with people from a different culture, it's important to find out about their nonverbal communication styles before you meet.

After You Read

How Well Did You Read?

Work with a partner. Read the statements. Write *T* (true) or *F* (false). Underline the information in the reading that supports your answer.

_____ 1. We communicate only by using words.

_____ 2. All cultures use the same nonverbal communication styles.

_____ 3. Pierre was not well-prepared for this business trip.

_____ 4. Difficulties with verbal communication led to misunderstandings between Pierre and the Japanese businessmen.

_____ 5. Pierre and the Japanese businessmen interpreted body language differently.

Check Your Understanding

A. Discuss Reading 2 with a partner. Take turns answering the questions.

1. What is nonverbal communication? Give two examples of nonverbal communication from Reading 2.

2. How do Japanese people feel about saying *no* directly, according to the reading? How do you feel about saying *no* directly?

3. Who was responsible for the communciation problem in Reading 2? Was it Pierre's fault? He was a guest in a different country. Or was it Mr. Tanaka's and Mr. Ataki's fault? Should they have understood Pierre's nonverbal communication style better? Explain your answer.

B. Read each question and circle the letter of the best answer.

1. What's the topic of paragraph 1?

   a. Clear communication between cultures
   b. Difficulties in communicating between cultures
   c. Verbal communication

2. Which statement is correct according to paragraph 1?

   a. Nonverbal communication is easier to understand than verbal communication.
   b. People from different countries use the same body language.
   c. People from different cultures sometimes find body language more confusing than verbal communication.

3. Pierre wasn't worried about communicating with the Japanese businessmen. Why?

   a. He has been to Japan many times before.
   b. He speaks Japanese.
   c. He could communicate through a translator.

4. Why does Pierre slap the businessmen on their backs?

   a. He is embarrassed.
   b. He thinks this is how you greet Japanese people.
   c. He is rude.
   d. He wants to show he is in charge.

5. What's the topic of paragraph 3?

   a. Pierre's body language
   b. Japanese body language
   c. Nonverbal communication causes problems.

6. Why does Pierre think Mr. Ataki is hiding something?

   a. Mr. Ataki is very quiet.
   b. Mr. Ataki takes a long time to answer.
   c. Mr. Ataki doesn't look at Pierre.
   d. Mr. Ataki nods.

7. Why did communication break down in this meeting?

   a. The men didn't understand each other's spoken language.
   b. The Japanese did not want to do business with Pierre's company.
   c. Their body language communicated confusing messages.
   d. The translator made mistakes.

8. What advice is given in the final paragraph?

   a. If you do business with people from a different culture, make sure you understand their nonverbal communication style before you meet.
   b. Make sure people from different cultures understand your body language before you meet so that they clearly understand you.
   c. Always take a translator with you to a business meeting.

Vocabulary Skill

Using Adjectives to Describe Feelings

Adjectives are words that describe nouns. Adjectives provide more information to the reader about people, places, or things. Adjectives that describe how someone is feeling often come after the verbs *to be, to feel,* and *to look.* Read these sentences. The underlined words are adjectives that describe feelings.

Because he was <u>embarrassed</u>, Pierre slapped the businessmen on the back.

Then there was silence, and Pierre felt <u>uncomfortable</u>.

The Japanese were <u>confused</u> by Pierre's behavior.

At the beginning of the meeting, Pierre looked <u>nervous</u>.

A. Read this list of adjectives and their definitions. Then answer the questions that follow, using adjectives from the list. Answer with complete sentences.

Word	Definition
awkward	not sure what to say or do because you are embarrassed
confident	knowing that you can do something well
comfortable	relaxed
confused	you cannot think clearly; you are not sure about something
depressed	very sad
embarrassed	ashamed in front of other people
excited	happy because something good happened or is going to happen
nervous	worried or frightened about something
relieved	feeling happy because something bad did not happen
self-conscious	worried about what you look like or what others think about you
shy	nervous and embarrassed about talking to people
uncomfortable	unable to relax because you are embarrassed or worried

1. How do you think Pierre felt before the meeting? Explain your answer.

   _____

2. How did he feel when he tried to shake hands with the businessmen?

   _____

3. How did the businessmen feel when Pierre slapped them on the back?

   _____

4. How do Western people feel when there is silence in a conversation? How do Japanese feel when there is silence?

   _____

5. How do you think Pierre felt at the end of his meeting? Explain your answer.

   _____

B. Discuss these questions with a partner. Then write the answers in complete sentences.

1. How would you feel if you arrived at a party on time but discovered you were the only person there?

   _____

2. How would you feel if your teacher asked you a question in class, you gave the wrong answer, and your classmates laughed?

_____

3. How would you feel if your teacher asked you to make eye contact when speaking to him or her?

_____

4. How would you feel if an American friend always asked, "How are you doing?" but didn't seem interested in your answer?

_____

Reading 3 *Brown Eyes–Blue Eyes*

Before You Read

Preview Reading 3 on pages 21 and 22. Read the title and look at the illustration. What do you think the story is going to be about? What do you think the title means?

Previewing Vocabulary

These words are in Reading 3. Read the words and their definitions. Then choose the best word to complete each sentence.

Word	Definition
adopt	to legally have someone else's child become part of your family
bright	intelligent, quick at learning
bundled up	dressed warmly
couple	two people who have a romantic relationship
dialect	a form of a language spoken in one area in a different way than it is spoken in other areas
disabled	cannot use a part of the body properly
land mines	bombs hidden below the ground that explode when someone or something goes over them
orphanage	home for children whose parents are dead
shadow	a dark shape that a person or an object makes when the light is blocked
suspicious	not trusting someone

1. The _____dialect_____ spoken in the northern part of the country is different from the language people speak in the southern part.

2. After World War II, many soldiers returned home ___disabled___ and could not work because of their injuries.

3. My friends are an unusual ___couple___. He is British and doesn't speak any Japanese. She is Japanese and only speaks a little English. However, they love each other very much!

4. It was so cold I ___bundled up___ my baby in two extra blankets.

5. My long, dark ___shadow___ on the ground told me the day was almost over. The sun would soon set.

6. In China, it is very unusual to find baby boys in a(n) ___orphanage___. There are many baby girls waiting to be adopted, however.

7. Even after the war, innocent children and citizens were injured and killed when they stepped on ___land mines___.

8. The police officer was very ___suspicious___ when he saw a man climbing out of a window. The man said he was getting a surprise present for his wife, but the officer didn't believe him.

9. Husbands and wives who cannot have children often try to ___adopt___ a child.

10. Most young children are naturally ___bright___. They love to learn, and they can learn an amazing amount very quickly.

Brown Eyes–Blue Eyes

1   Nobody knew where the child came from. At least no one knew exactly where he was from. He was left on the bullet-scarred steps of an orphanage in a small town in northern Cambodia. A French nurse who worked at the orphanage found him on New Year's Eve. He was bundled up in a brightly colored cotton blanket like a gift to welcome in the coming year.

2   He was a small boy, thin and pale. The doctor thought he was about two years old, but he looked half his age. There was no note. No one knew his parents. No one knew his name. "Another lost boy," thought one of the nurses as she gently bathed him.

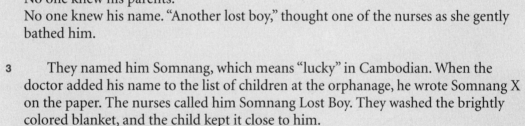

3   They named him Somnang, which means "lucky" in Cambodian. When the doctor added his name to the list of children at the orphanage, he wrote Somnang X on the paper. The nurses called him Somnang Lost Boy. They washed the brightly colored blanket, and the child kept it close to him.

4   In the next two years, Somnang Lost Boy grew to be a handsome child. He had dark, almost black hair, olive skin, and the bluest eyes in Cambodia—blue eyes in a land of brown-eyed people, blue eyes just like his father who had long ago returned to England, or France, or America.

5   He was also a bright child. He learned quickly. He understood the French spoken at the orphanage and the local dialect. He understood, but he never spoke, not a word. The doctors said there was nothing wrong with him. "Be patient," the doctor said. "He'll talk when he's ready."

continued

6   From time to time, European families who wanted to adopt a child visited the orphanage. They visited and left with a child. The nurses called these Happy-Sad days because for every child who began a new life, many more were left behind: the older children with hard, <u>suspicious</u> eyes, the disabled children injured from land mines left over from an almost forgotten war, the "different" children who lived inside their own heads, and Somnang Lost Boy, the one who never spoke.

7   Another Happy-Sad day arrived. A couple came into the courtyard where the children were playing. The babies were sleeping in the shade of the fig tree. The older children looked up from their game and moved silently to the wall. The man was very tall and very blond. The woman looked tiny next to him. "She looks Japanese," thought the nurse as she <u>led</u> the couple across the yard.

8   Somnang looked up as a shadow fell across his space. The man towered above him. The woman quietly sat down next to him. Using her finger, she traced a smiling face in the dust. Then she smiled at him. He sat very still, his blue eyes fixed on the ground. She began to talk in a language he didn't understand. As she talked, the tall blond man sat down next to her. Somnang reached for a corner of his blanket and held it tightly.

9   The couple came back the next day. On the third day, the woman had a book. She opened it and showed Somnang pictures of smiling people. Many of the pictures were of the man and the woman and a young girl smiling as she held their hands. Somnang touched the pictures with one hand while his other hand held onto the blanket.

10   The couple visited every day for two weeks. On the last day, the doctors and the nurses and the cooks came into the courtyard. The woman walked over to Somnang Lost Boy and held out her hand. She smiled at him, and his blue eyes looked up at her. He took her hand, and she took the hand of her husband. Together they walked out of the orphanage, the brightly colored blanket trailing in the dust. Somnang Lost Boy had found his dark-blond, tall-short, Eastern-Western, brown eyed-blue eyed family.

After You Read

How Well Did You Read?

Read the statements. Write *T* (true) or *F* (false). Underline the information in the reading that supports your answer.

___T___ 1. The child was left on the steps by unknown parents.

___F___ 2. The boy looked like other Cambodian children.

_____ 3. Not all of the children were adopted from the orphanage.

_____ 4. The boy was named after his mother.

_____ 5. The boy was adopted by a family who lived nearby.

Check Your Understanding

A. Discuss Reading 3 with a partner. Take turns answering the questions.

1. Why do you think the boy's mother left him on the steps of the orphanage?

2. Somnang was healthy, but he didn't talk. Why do you think he kept silent?

3. Which children were not adopted? Why were they not adopted?

4. Why do you think Somnang kept his blanket close to him?

5. This story is about international adoptions. Do you think children from one country should be adopted by parents from a different country and culture? Explain your answer.

B. Answer the questions. Use complete sentences.

1. Why did the nurses name him Somnang Lost Boy?

   _____

2. In this story, we learn that Cambodia has had a war. What two details tell us this?

   _____

3. What are the Happy-Sad days, and why are they called this?

   _____

4. What do we learn about Somnang's birth parents?

   _____

5. What do we know about Somnang's adopted family?

   _____

continued

6. Why do you think the woman showed Somnang the photographs?

_____

7. Why is the blanket important to Somnang?

_____

Vocabulary Skill

Using Words from Other Languages

A language is a living thing. It constantly changes. One way a language changes is by adding words from a different language. English uses many words that come from other languages. As the world becomes more global and people travel and communicate with more people from other countries, languages will continue to change. More "non-English" words will be added to English, and more English words will be used in other languages.

A. Work with a partner. Match the words to the language they came from. If you are not sure, check your dictionary.

_____ **1.** kindergarten (school for 4–5-year-old children)

a. Japanese

_____ **2.** confetti (small pieces of paper thrown at parties and parades)

b. Turkish

_____ **3.** karaoke (singing along with music)

c. German

_____ **4.** kayak (a type of small boat usually for one person)

d. Italian

_____ **5.** yogurt (a thick liquid made from milk)

e. Native American

B. Work with a partner to answer the questions.

1. Write three words from your first language that most English speakers understand. See if your partner knows what they mean.

a. _____

b. _____

c. _____

2. Now write three English words that are easily understood in other countries. One example is _Internet._

a. _____

b. _____

c. _____

Expanding the Topic

Connecting Reading with Writing

A. On a separate sheet of paper, answer the questions in complete sentences. Use ideas and vocabulary that you have learned in the readings and exercises.

1. Have you ever had communication problems in the country where you are now living? What happened? How did you feel?

2. If you have moved to a new country, or visited for a long time, how did you feel about talking with native speakers when you first arrived? How do you feel about it today?

3. How do you feel about talking to other students in your class? How do you feel about talking to your teacher?

4. If you have moved to a new country, or visited for a long time, did you find any customs strange when you first came to this country? Explain why they seemed strange.

5. What customs should visitors know about if they go to your country?

B. Write a paragraph about one of the following topics.

1. Imagine you are one of the parents adopting Somnang. Your daughter is at home staying with grandparents while you are in Cambodia. Write a letter to her describing your first few days with Somnang at the orphanage. Use details from the story to make your letter interesting. Explain to your daughter how you feel and how you think Somnang feels.

2. Families have changed a lot in the past fifty years. You've just read a story about a family adopting a child from a different country. What other different kinds of families are there today? Describe some different families. Discuss their differences and similarities.

3. Think about your grandparents' family and your family today. How has your family changed in the past two or three generations?

4. Choose one of these topics and write a paragraph. You can use the topic as the first sentence of your paragraph. Use information and ideas from the readings and the exercises to make your writing interesting. You may need to do some research before you write. For example, you may need to walk around your neighborhood to find out what kind of shops and businesses it has. Or you might need to interview your teacher to find information for the last topic.

   - My group is like a small global village.

   - My neighborhood is like a global village.

   - I am a member of the global village.

   - My teacher is a member of the global village.

Exploring Online

Life Skill

Searching for Information on the Internet

The World Wide Web, also known as the Web, is the part of the Internet that contains information from millions of sources around the world. This information is organized into Web sites. Because there is so much information on the Web, it is an excellent resource. However, it can also be confusing. A search engine will help you find the information you need. To use a search engine, follow these steps:

1. Go online so you are connected to the Internet.

2. Type in the Web address of a major search engine such as www.google.com, www.yahoo.com, or www.msn.com.

3. The home or front page of the search engine will come up on your screen. Now think about the information you need. Think of the key (most important) words.

4. Type these words into the search box. Be as specific as you can.

5. The search engine finds articles or Web sites that contain these words and will list them on your screen. The articles that are most closely related to your topic will be listed first.

6. Click on an article or Web site you think might be helpful, and it will appear on your screen.

Answer the questions using the Internet. If you need help with the computer, or have questions about doing an Internet search, ask your teacher or a classmate to help you.

1. The last reading took place in Cambodia. Go online and use one of the major search engines to search for information about Cambodia. Use *Cambodia* as the search word and answer the following questions:

   a. What is the population of Cambodia? _____

   b. What is the name of its capital? _____

   c. What languages do people speak in Cambodia? _____

   _____

   d. What is one problem this country faces in the future? _____

   _____

   _____

   Web address or addresses used: _____

   _____

2. While you have been reading this first chapter, you have been getting to know some of the other students in your class. Choose one student who is from a different country or city than you. Use the name of this country or city as the search word, and find out five facts about it.

Country / City: _____

a. _____

b. _____

c. _____

d. _____

e. _____

Web address or addresses used: _____

3. A student in your class wants to visit the country or city where you were born. She wants to prepare well. She asks you to find one or two Web sites that will give her good information about this place. Use the name of the country or city as a search word, and find Web sites that give accurate information and have good pictures. Write down the names of the Web sites. Explain why you think these are good sites for her to use.

Web address: _____.

This is a good site because _____

_____.

Web address: _____.

This is a good site because _____

_____.

Safety Matters

Chapter 2 describes several emergency situations. Readings 1 and 2 are about fire safety. Reading 3 is a story about an accident that happened at a workplace.

In this chapter, you will practice:

Reading Skills

→ Previewing a reading

→ Finding main ideas

→ Predicting

→ Scanning for details

→ Recognizing a sequence of events

Vocabulary Skills

→ Using context clues to understand vocabulary

→ Using suffixes: *-ful* and *-less*

Life Skills

→ Planning an escape route

→ Completing an accident report

Before You Read

Previewing

Discuss the questions with a partner.

1. Read the title. What do you think *Fire Safety 101* means?

2. Look at the illustrations. What is happening in each picture? Have you ever been in any of these situations? What did you do?

3. The emergency telephone number in the United States is 911. How do you call for emergency services in other countries?

4. Have you ever called the emergency number here or in another country? Why? What happened?

Vocabulary Skill

Using Context Clues to Understand Vocabulary

When you read, you don't need to look up every new word in a dictionary, and you don't need to know the exact meaning of every word. You can often guess the meaning of new words through **context.** The context is the words and sentences around the new word. There are several kinds of context clues that can help you understand new vocabulary.

1. **Look at the meaning of the sentence as a whole.**

   At three o'clock in the morning, the <u>residents</u> of Ashton Apartments were sleeping soundly.

   Residents are the people who live in the apartments.

2. **Look for a definition of the new word. A dash, parentheses, or a comma can introduce a definition.**

   Some fires are <u>inevitable</u>—you cannot completely stop all fires.

   Inevitable means something you can't stop from happening.

3. **Look for examples. Words that introduce examples include *such as, for example,* and *for instance.***

   Keep <u>flammable</u> materials, such as gas and paint, outside the house in a safe container.

   Flammable materials burn easily.

The words in bold print are in Reading 1 on page 32. Use context clues and circle the letter of the answer closest in meaning to the word(s) in bold print.

1. In a fire, children are most **at risk.** For example, they are in danger because they panic in frightening situations and may not know what to do.

   a. likely to cry
   b. likely to be hurt
   c. will take chances

2. People with children should keep medicine **out of reach.** Children who take adult medicine can get very sick.

   a. where it is easy to find quickly
   b. where it is difficult to get to
   c. nearby

3. It is not safe to leave small children **unattended** in a locked car. There should always be an adult in the car with young children.

   a. alone
   b. bored
   c. playing with friends

4. Unfortunately, many people die every year because of fires; however, many people are also saved **annually** by firefighters.

   a. often
   b. sometimes
   c. every year

5. It is possible to **prevent** a heart attack by exercising regularly and eating healthy food, including lots of vegetables and fruit.

   a. improve
   b. cause
   c. stop from happening

6. The landlord told me all the **appliances**—stove, refrigerator, and dishwasher— worked. However, when I turned on the stove, it made a very strange noise and I smelled something burning.

   a. wiring and plumbing
   b. stereos and televisions
   c. electrical or gas machines in a house

7. More and more people are wearing seat belts in their cars. As a result, the number of serious car injuries has **decreased**.

   a. risen
   b. fallen
   c. remained the same

8. **Senior citizens** today enjoy an active life. For example, many people in their seventies and eighties swim, play golf, and go walking or jogging.

   a. active people
   b. grandparents
   ✓ c. older people

9. When **the power went out,** there were no lights and no heat in the classroom. Finally, the teacher told the students they could go home.

   a. there was a lightning storm
   ✓ b. there was no electricity
   c. the teacher turned off the power

10. I need to **install** new smoke detectors in my house because the old ones are all broken.

    a. fix
    ✓ b. put up and connect
    c. turn off

11. **Commercial** buildings, such as restaurants or factories, are required by law to have a sprinkler system that automatically releases water if it senses smoke.

    a. apartment
    ✓ b. business
    c. school

12. Safety experts believe it is **essential** to check the batteries in smoke detectors twice a year. You must do this to be sure that the detectors work correctly.

    a. not necessary
    b. safe
    ✓ c. very important

Now Read

Fire Safety 101 # grup

1   There are about 24 million fires every year in the United States. These fires cause over $11 billion in damage. Unfortunately, about 6,000 people die every year in fires. Many of these are senior citizens or children who cannot move quickly or do not know what to do. In addition, 100,000 people are injured in fires annually. We can't stop all fires. However, careful planning reduces the number of fires and increases the chances of people surviving fires.

2   People can prevent fires by following several simple rules. Check that electrical appliances like stoves and dishwashers are safe. Keep flammable materials, such as spare gasoline and extra paint, outside the house in a safe container. Never leave a burning candle unattended, and never let children play with matches or lighters. In fact, adults should always keep matches out of children's reach. Smokers should never smoke in bed, since many fires begin with people falling asleep while they are smoking. Most importantly, install smoke detectors on every level of your apartment or house. Every residence should have a smoke detector in each bedroom, at the top of the stairs, and near the kitchen. Check the batteries in smoke detectors twice a year.

3   Unfortunately, accidents will happen and fires will occur. Knowing what to do in a fire can save lives and prevent injuries. Safety experts stress the importance of making a fire escape plan and practicing that plan. This is essential if there are children living in the home, since they are most at risk. Children often panic easily and get confused in a frightening situation. In fact, firefighters have reported finding children hiding in a closet or under a bed in a burning house. Residents need to plan two escape routes out of the house, and then practice that plan in daylight and in the dark in case the power goes out.

4   These days, prevention is an important part of fire safety. Many fire departments have a fire safety officer who goes to schools and communities and talks to people about fire safety. Some fire stations hand out free smoke alarms, and some cities have even built model homes where children can practice getting out of smoke-filled buildings. Schools are required to practice fire drills, and commercial buildings, like stores and offices, must meet safety standards. Because of this emphasis on prevention, the number of fires has decreased. By continuing to follow simple rules and by practicing their escape plans, people can continue to reduce the number of fires.

After You Read

How Well Did You Read?

Read the statements. Write *T* (true), *F* (false), or *N* (not enough information).
Underline the information in the reading that supports your answer.

_N_ 1. Most people who are killed in fires are either very young or very old.

_F_ 2. According to the reading, all fires can be prevented.

_F_ 3. According to the reading, you should install a smoke detector in the kitchen.

_F_ 4. Children remain calm in dangerous situations like fires.

_N_ 5. The number of fires has gone down in the last few years.

Check Your Understanding

Work in small groups. Discuss the questions, and share your ideas with the class.

1. Reading 1 recommends checking batteries in smoke detectors twice a year. Does your house or apartment have smoke detectors? When was the last time you checked the batteries? Where can you buy a smoke detector?

2. Paragraph 2 suggests several things you can do to prevent fires. What are they? Can you think of any other ways to prevent fires?

3. Look around your classroom. Is there any information on the walls about fire safety? Is there a sprinkler system? Is there an alarm? What would you do if you heard someone shout "Fire!"? Where would be a good place to meet outside the building?

Finding Main Ideas

In Chapter 1 you learned how to find the topic of a paragraph. The topic is the general idea. A paragraph also has a **main idea**—what the writer wants to say about the topic.

You can find main ideas by asking two questions:

- What is the general topic?
- What does the writer say about the topic?

The general idea, or topic, is a word or phrase. The main idea, or what the writer wants to say about the topic, is expressed as a complete sentence. For example, reread paragraph 2 of Reading 1 on page 32.

> The topic is "preventing fires."

> The main idea is "People can prevent fires by following several simple rules."

Read each paragraph and answer the questions. As you read, try to guess the meaning of words without using a dictionary.

1.   "911. Are you reporting an emergency?" This is how the emergency dispatcher, or operator, answers dozens of 911 calls each day. Sometimes the caller is reporting an accident. Sometimes a neighbor is complaining about noise. In fact, there are many reasons why people call 911. The majority of 911 calls are because of illness or injury. A worried mother calls because her child has a high fever, or a daughter calls because her elderly father has fallen. Other 911 calls report fires or accidents. Now that most people have cell phones, several people often call in to report the same accident. Finally, 911 is used to report crimes. People report that their car has been stolen or their house has been burglarized. Whatever the emergency, the 911 dispatcher is waiting calmly to take your call.

What is the topic? _____ Call 911 _____

What is the main idea? _How the emergency dispatcher or operator answers dozens of 911 calls each day..._

2.   On September 11, 2001, the world witnessed the amazing bravery of firefighters. Millions of people watched the terrible events of that day live on television. TV viewers saw people running out of the Twin Towers in New York, away from the smoke and the flames. Viewers saw firefighters running into the building toward the fire. Even firefighters who weren't on duty that day came from their homes to help in the rescue attempt. And when the dust began to settle, and day turned to night, firefighters continued to work to find the injured. Since September 11, 2001, Americans look at this remarkable group of men and women with a new respect.

What is the topic? _____ The world witnessed 2001 ____

What is the main idea? _____

_____

3.   Most days are busy for a firefighter. Early in the morning, a firefighter begins his twenty-four-hour shift with the rest of his crew. In Station 16X in San Francisco, the crew of three men and one woman meets with their lieutenant to discuss plans for the day. Training for different emergencies never stops. Today, the crew is going to take another EMT (emergency medical training) course. They will learn how to use new equipment to save the lives of heart attack victims. After the training, one member of the crew will cook lunch while the others check equipment. In the afternoon, they'll practice earthquake drills. After dinner, the lieutenant has arranged for the crew to visit a local community center to talk about fire safety with children. Of course, at any time during the day, the crew can be called out for an emergency. In fact, many firefighters are called out up to ten times a day. A firefighter's life is always busy.

What is the topic? _____

What is the main idea? _A fire fighter's life is always busy.___

4.   Because the fire department must get to an emergency as quickly as possible, there are rules to protect both the firefighters and other drivers. Firefighters use lights and sirens to respond to a 911 call. By law, drivers must move to the right side of the road when they hear the sirens. As an engine races through a red light, cars in front must move quickly to the right to get out of its way. However, sometimes drivers don't follow the rules. For example, last week, the crew of Engine 2X noticed a red pickup truck following them. As the fire truck raced through a red light, the pickup truck followed. Two young men

continued

were in the truck, and the firefighters could see them laughing as they drove behind the fire engine. The crew of Engine 2X radioed to the police for assistance, and within a short period of time, a police car pulled the truck over. The young men were fined $500 for dangerous driving. Hopefully the young men will remember next time: Sirens and lights—move to the right.

What is the topic? _Sirens and lights – move to the right_

What is the main idea? _The fire department must get to the emergency as quickly as possible._

Fire Safety at Ashton Apartments

Before You Read

Reading Skill	
	Predicting
	In Chapter 1, you got a general idea of the topic by looking at the titles, headings, and illustrations. **Predicting** is guessing what the writer will say after looking at the titles, headings, and illustrations. Predicting helps you understand the reading more easily. As you read, check to see if your predictions were correct.

An apartment manager has developed a flyer to improve safety for the residents. Before you read the flyer, think about the safety information you learned from Reading 1. Use this information to predict three safety ideas you think will be included in the flyer.

1. _____

2. _____

3. _____

Using Context Clues to Understand Vocabulary

The words in bold print are in Reading 2 on page 38. Work with a partner and guess the meanings of these words without using a dictionary. Write the meanings in your own words.

1. There will be a **fire drill** three times a year. This will give you an opportunity to practice what to do in case of a fire.

   fire drill: _____

2. **Replace** batteries in smoke detectors twice a year. If you don't replace them, your smoke detector might not work when you need it.

   replace: _____*Check*_____

3. Do not try to **extinguish** a fire that is growing very quickly. Instead, get away from it as quickly as possible and call 911.

   extinguish: _____

4. If you have time, **warn** your neighbors about the fire. Bang hard on their doors and shout "Fire!"

   warn: _____

5. Don't run. Don't **panic.** Think clearly. Stay calm.

   panic: _____

6. You **set off** some alarms by pressing a bell; you start other alarms by pulling a handle or lever.

   set off: _____

Ashton Apartments

Fire Safety Information for All Residents

Please take the time to read this safety information, and share it with your family. There will be a fire drill three times a year. This will give you an opportunity to practice fire safety.

What you should do to be prepared:

1. Make sure your apartment has smoke detectors.
2. Replace smoke detector batteries twice a year, when you set your clocks for Daylight Savings Time or Standard Time.
3. Plan and practice escape routes from each room.
4. Choose a safe meeting place outside the building.
5. Keep a fire extinguisher in the kitchen, and make sure all household members can use it.
6. If there are children in the household, talk to them about fire safety. Practice the plan with them.
7. Keep items such as clothing away from heaters.
8. Do not keep flammable items, such as gas and paint, in the apartment.

What you should do in case of fire:

1. Don't run. Don't panic. Think clearly. Stay calm.
2. Tell everyone in your apartment there is a fire.
3. If you see or smell smoke, cover your mouth and nose with a wet cloth. Get down on your hands and knees, and follow your escape route.
4. Feel the base of the door before you open it. If the door is hot, do not open it. Go out through the window if you live on the first floor. If you live on a high floor, put a towel at the base of the door, and go to a window. Wait for help.
5. Do not attempt to extinguish a fire that is rapidly growing.
6. If you have time, warn your neighbors about the fire.
7. Set off a fire alarm. There is one on every floor next to the stairs.
8. Use the stairs; never use the elevator.
9. Once you are out of the building, go to the parking lots.
10. Call 911 as soon as you can.
11. Stay out of the building. Don't go back inside until the fire department tells you it is safe.

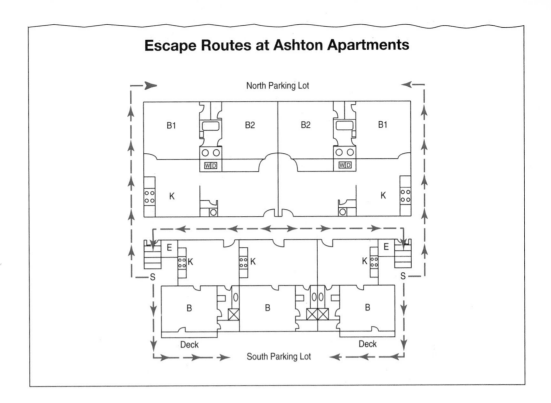

Escape Routes at Ashton Apartments

After You Read

How Well Did You Read?

Work with a partner. Read the statements. Write *T* (true), *F* (false), or *N* (not enough information). Underline the information in the reading that supports your answer.

_F_ **1.** There is a fire drill twice a year.

_T_ **2.** The whole family should practice fire safety.

_____ **3.** The flyer was written after Ashton Apartments had a bad fire.

_F_ **4.** People should always go out into their hallway if there is a fire.

_F_ **5.** Residents should try to put out the fire before calling 911.

Check Your Understanding

Work with a partner. Think about Reading 2, look at the escape routes, and take turns answering the questions about Ashton Apartments.

1. How do you get out of a bedroom?

2. How do you get out of a kitchen?

3. When is it okay to go back inside the building?

4. What do you do if you are in an apartment and the door to the hallway is very hot?

Scanning for Details

Sometimes you read to find a detail rather than the main idea. To find a detail, you don't need to read the complete text. You can **scan,** or quickly look for the details. When you scan for details,

- decide what information you need.
- identify key words to help find this information.
- remember the key words and quickly move your eyes down the page. Don't read as you scan. Just look for the key words.
- read the sentences around the key words to be sure you have found the correct information.

Example:

Question:	According to Reading 2, how often is there a fire drill?
Information needed:	*how often there is a fire drill*
Key words:	*how often* and *fire drill*
Answer:	Three times a year

Read the questions. Underline the key words in the question. Then scan Reading 2 for the answers.

1. When should residents check batteries in smoke detectors?

   Two times a year, when you set your clocks for Daylight Savings Time or Standard Time

2. Where should residents keep a fire extinguisher?

   They should keep in the kitchen.

3. Where are the fire alarms located?

   The fire alarms locate on every floor on the stairs

4. Where should residents meet outside of the building?

   _____

5. How should residents prepare children for a fire?

   _____

Using Context Clues to Understand Vocabulary

Complete the sentences with words from the list. If you are not sure which word to use, go back to Reading 2, scan for the word, and read the sentences to understand its meaning.

calm	√make sure	set off — *зажечать*
extinguish	√panic	√ smoke detector
fire extinguisher	√rapidly	√warn
√household		

1. You should change the batteries in your _smoke detector_ twice a year.

2. Don't _panic_. Take a deep breath, and try to think clearly.

3. When I heard the fire alarm, I banged on my neighbor's door to _warn_ her about the fire.

4. He _set off_ the fire alarm when he smelled smoke.

5. Everyone should keep a _fire extinguisher_ in the kitchen in case a fire breaks out.

6. Firefighters are usually very _calm_, even when they are in a dangerous situation.

7. Please _make sure_ you know where the fire alarm is.

8. Hiroki made sure that all members of his _household_ knew where the fire extinguisher was and understood how to get out of the house quickly.

9. The fire was so hot that James didn't try to _extinguish_ it. Instead, he left the house and called 911.

10. Because the weather was so dry, the fire spread _rapidly_.

Life Skill

Planning an Escape Route

Firefighters and other safety experts believe it is very important to plan and practice an escape route. An escape route can prevent injuries if there is a fire or another emergency such as an earthquake. All members of the household should know and practice this escape route.

Using the floor plan on page 39 to help you, complete the following activities.

1. On a piece of paper, draw a plan of the house or apartment you live in. Clearly mark the different rooms, windows, and doors.

2. Use arrows to indicate your escape route. Label your drawing "My Escape Route."

3. Describe your escape route to a partner.

Reading 3   *Be Safe, Not Sorry!*

Before You Read

Making Predictions

Reading 3 on pages 43 to 47 is about an accident that happened at a workplace. Before you start reading, do the following tasks with a partner.

1. Look at the illustrations on pages 43, 44, and 45. Describe what is happening in each picture.

2. Read the safety rules poster on page 45 aloud to your partner.

3. Make three predictions about what you think will happen in this story:

a. _____

b. _____

c. _____

Using Context Clues to Understand Vocabulary

The words in bold print are in Reading 3. Read each sentence and guess the meaning. Write the meaning in your own words.

1. My father works a night **shift,** so he goes to work just as I am going to bed. Next month he will start on the day shift and will have better hours.

   shift: _____

2. I worked ten hours **overtime** last week. The extra money will be helpful, but working a fifty-hour week is very tiring.

   overtime: _____

3. Would you **do** me **a favor** and pick up my son from child care? I can't get him because I have a dentist appointment.

   do . . . a favor: _____

4. The store manager hired more people because she didn't want to be **understaffed** during the busy holiday season.

understaffed: _____not enough people on the work_

5. When the accident happened, the day shift manager had already left. The night shift manager was **on duty,** and he helped the injured employee.

on duty: _____

6. Do not **overload** the forklift. Load to the safety line only.

overload: _____

7. You should always look behind you before you **reverse** your car.

reverse: _____

8. Yesterday, a young boy ran out in front of my car. Luckily I managed to **avoid** hitting him, but I crashed into another car. No one was injured.

avoid: _____

upencamne?

Now Read

Be Safe, Not Sorry!

continued

1   DIY is a large home improvement store. DIY stands for "do it yourself." The store attracts people who enjoy fixing up their homes and yards. DIY employs about fifty people. The employees unload deliveries, stock shelves, and help customers at the cash registers. There is always a manager on duty.

2   Most employees like working at DIY. The hourly wage is good, and after three months, full-time employees get health and dental benefits. There are also three shifts available: day, swing, and night. The swing shift, which begins at 4:00 P.M. and ends at 1:00 A.M., is popular with students from the nearby community college. For many of the workers, however, the best thing about working at DIY is the overtime. Employees are paid time and a half for overtime, so their monthly salary can quickly increase with this extra money.

3   It was early April and the weather was unusually warm. DIY was full of people buying new lawn mowers and plants to brighten up the yard after a long, gray winter. That Saturday, Maria was the manager on duty. She was at her desk, and she was worried. She picked up the shop intercom.

4   "Vlad and Andy, please come to the office. Thank you."

5   Her voice was clearly heard throughout the store, and two employees looked up at the same time. Vlad was unloading boxes of gardening tools and putting them on shelves. Andy was helping a customer load sheets of plywood onto a large cart. Both men went to the office. Maria smiled at them. "Hi guys. How's it going?"

continued

6   Vlad smiled back, but he looked tired and hot. He sat down and rubbed his neck. "Everything's fine, Maria. Boy, it's busy out there. We must have half the city in the store today," he replied.

7   Andy kept quiet, but nodded in agreement.

8   "Well, that's what I wanted to talk about," Maria said. "Jim and Tracy have just called in sick for today's swing shift. Would you two do us a favor and work some extra hours? I don't want to be understaffed when we are so busy."

9   Vlad sighed. "I don't know, boss. I've already worked a lot of overtime this week. My wife hardly recognizes me anymore. And, to tell you the truth, I'm really tired today."

10   "Come on, Vlad. I can give you time and a half and an extra day off next week. We've got new deliveries coming in, and I must get everything on the shelves before tomorrow's rush begins. Just work until ten."

continued

11   Vlad thought about the car payments and the new baby that was on the way. He looked over at Andy, who nodded. "Okay, Maria, but at ten o'clock, we're out of here."

12   "Thanks, guys." Maria said.

13   Vlad and Andy were busy with customers most of the evening. At nine thirty, Vlad finally went out to the back of the store and got the forklift. As he started it up, he glanced at the safety rules posted on the wall.

14   Vlad reached down and put on his hard hat. By now he had a painful headache, and he was hot and thirsty. Carefully looking behind him, he reversed the forklift and got his first load of plywood sheets. When he drove back into the store, Andy helped him unload the plywood onto the shelves. Before Vlad went back to get more, he called to Andy, "You should put on your hat, Andy. If the boss sees you, you'll be in trouble."

15   Andy nodded.

16   Vlad went back for more plywood. It was now 9:45. They had another three loads before they were finished and could go home. "I'm not going to get out of here until midnight," he thought. So he made a decision. He loaded two piles of plywood. The plywood was now ten inches over the safety line. Vlad then drove carefully back into the store. He noticed Andy was still not wearing his hat, but Vlad was too tired to care.

17   Andy raised his eyebrows when he saw how much wood Vlad had loaded, but he didn't say anything.

18   Andy reached up to get the first piece of plywood. The pile was so high he first had to climb on the forklift to reach it. Vlad leaned over from the driver's seat to help. Just then, the whole pile of plywood moved. It was too heavy. The top two sheets began to slide off. "Look out, Andy!" Vlad yelled.

19   But it was too late. Andy tried to step out of the way, but he caught his foot in the forklift. As he fell, he managed to avoid the falling plywood, but he hit his head heavily against the concrete floor. To Vlad's horror, Andy lay motionless on the floor.

continued

20   Vlad jumped down. He grabbed his radio and called for help. Maria had already left, and the swing shift manager ran to where Andy was lying on the floor. He ordered Vlad to call an ambulance. Medics from the fire station arrived a few minutes later and took Andy to the hospital.

21   Vlad wanted to go with his friend, but the manager wouldn't let him. As soon as the ambulance pulled away, the manager called him over. "Vlad, you need to fill out paperwork before you go home. Come up to the office."

22   Vlad followed him. He felt terrible. It was his fault that Andy was hurt. All he could think about was his friend lying in the ambulance. How badly was he hurt? Was he going to be okay? The manager handed him an accident report form. Vlad closed his eyes for a minute and then began to fill it out.

After You Read

How Well Did You Read?

Read the statements. Write *T* (true), *F* (false), or *N* (not enough information). Underline the information in the reading that supports your answer.

_____T_____ **1.** Maria asked Vlad and Andy to work extra hours because the store was busy and she was understaffed.

_____F_____ **2.** Vlad and Andy were excited to work overtime.

_____F_____ **3.** Vlad overloaded the forklift because he wanted to leave at 10:00 P.M.

_____F_____ **4.** Vlad thought the accident was Andy's fault because he wasn't wearing a hat.

_____N_____ **5.** The manager thought the accident was Vlad's fault.

Check Your Understanding

A. **Discuss the questions in groups. Then report your answers to the class.**

Vlad, Andy, and the manager were all partly responsible for this accident. Who do you think has the most responsibility for the accident? Who has the least responsibility? Why?

B. **Answer the following questions in complete sentences. Use your own words and words from Reading 3.**

1. Who likes to shop at DIY?

   <u>People who like to fix things themselves shop at DIY.</u>

2. Why do you think students like to work at DIY?

   <u>Students need to earn some money for tuition</u>

3. Why did Maria ask the two men to work overtime?

   <u>She didn't want to be understaffed when the store was busy.</u>

4. Why did Vlad agree to work overtime?

   <u>Vlad thought about the car payments and the new baby that was on the way.</u>

5. Why were Vlad and Andy late in unloading the plywood?

   <u>They were too tired.</u>

6. Did Andy follow the safety rules? Why or why not?

   <u>Andy didn't follow the safety rules. He should put on his hat</u>

7. How did Andy get hurt? <u>Andy reach up to get the first piece of plywood. The pile was so high he first had to climb on the on the forklift to reach it.</u>

8. Why didn't the manager allow Vlad to go to the hospital with his friend? <u>Vlad need to fill out paperwork before he left work.</u>

Recognizing a Sequence of Events

A **sequence** is a series of events or steps that follow one another. Readings that describe events or tell how to do something are organized in a sequence. Recognizing the sequence helps you understand the reading. Words such as *first, next, before, then, after, as, at the same time, later, as soon as,* and *finally* show that the reading is organized as a sequence. Words that show time and dates also show sequence.

Example:

At **nine-thirty**, Vlad **finally** went out to the back of the store and got the forklift.

Before Vlad went back to get more, he called to Andy, "You should put on your hat, Andy. If the boss sees you, you'll be in trouble."

A sequence of events led to Andy's accident. Look at the list of some of the most important events. Other events have been left out. Read the list carefully, and add the important events that are not included. Go back and reread parts of the story if you need to. When you finish, compare your list with a partner's.

1. Two employees called in sick.

2. _____

3. Vlad and Andy agreed to work that evening.

4. Vlad and Andy were very busy with customers.

5. _____

6. Vlad drove the first load of plywood to Andy, and they unloaded it.

7. _____

8. Vlad and Andy tried to unload the plywood.

9. _____

10. Andy tried to move out of the way.

11. _____

12. Vlad called the manager on his radio.

13. _____

14. The medics arrived.

15. _____

Using Suffixes: -ful and -less

A **suffix** is a letter or letters that you add to the end of a word. A suffix changes the part of speech of the word. For example, it can change the word from a noun to an adjective, or a verb to an adverb. Sometimes a suffix also changes the meaning of the word.

> To Vlad's horror, Andy lay **motionless** on the floor.

To form the adjective *motionless,* add the suffix *-less* to the noun *motion. Motionless* means "without motion."

> By now he had a **painful** headache, and he was hot and thirsty.

To form the adjective *painful,* add the suffix *-ful* to the noun *pain. Painful* means "full of pain."

A. Read the words with the suffix *-less*. Then choose the best word to complete each sentence.

careless	~~painless~~	senseless	useless
fearless	penniless	thoughtless	worthless

1. The doctor said to the woman, "Don't worry. This won't hurt at all. It's a
   _____ painless _____ procedure."

2. My ten-year-old brother is not afraid of anything. He's ___ fearless ___.

3. ___ Thoughtless ___ people never take the time to think about other people.

4. I bought a painting because I thought it was valuable. Unfortunately, it turned out to be ___ worthless ___.

5. The homeless woman held a sign that said "Please help. I'm ___ penniless ___."

6. Violence is often ___ senseless ___. There is no reason for it.

7. The campers were ___ careless ___ and didn't put out their campfire. As a result, the forest caught on fire.

8. This new pen is ___ useless ___. It doesn't work at all.

B. Look at the words with the suffix *-ful*. They mean the opposite of the words with the suffix *-less*. Complete the sentences below in your own words.

-ful	-less
careful	careless
fearful	fearless
painful	painless
thoughtful	thoughtless
useful	useless

1. Because he's a careful driver, he _drives without any accident_.

2. It's very painful when you _hurt someones feelings._ .

3. Ten-year-old boys are often fearless. They _don't understand that something can be dangerous_

4. A _dictionary_ is very useful if you want to improve your English.

5. My daughter is very thoughtful. Every morning she _cooks a breakfast_

6. My neighbor is often very careless. Yesterday he _fell down on the street_.

7. John is fearful of many things. He is even _scared of walking in the dark_.

8. My sister is so thoughtless, she _buys a lot of things._ .

Life Skill

Completing an Accident Report

After any accident at work, employees must complete accident reports. There are usually two reports. One is completed by the employee who was involved in the accident. The second is completed by that person's supervisor or manager. These reports should clearly describe what happened and should help the company prevent more accidents in the future.

A. The manager at DIY gave the following accident report form to Vlad and told him to complete it. Imagine you are Vlad. Read it carefully. Use the information from Reading 3 to complete the report. Be as clear as you can. When you finish, share your answers with a partner.

DIY Employee Accident Report

Note: This must be completed within twenty-four hours of the accident.

Date of accident: _04. 01. 06_

Time of accident: _9:50_

Name of person completing form: _Vlad_

Name of person injured: _Andy_

Type of treatment: Check (✓) all that apply.

○ None

○ DIY first aid

✓ Ambulance

✓ Hospital

What happened?

Be brief and as clear as possible. Do not write about the causes of the accident. Do not write about who is to blame. Just describe the accident.

Andy and I were loading and unloading plywood when _I decided to load two piles of plywood. Then I drove back into the store and I noticed that Andy wasn't wearing his hat. When Andy climbed on the forklift to reach the plywood, the two top sheets of plywood slided off. Andy tried to jump out of the way, but he caught his foot in the forklift and feel on the ground. When he feel on the ground, he hit his head against the floor._

Signature of person completing the form: _____

B. **Now read the Manager's Investigation Report and do the following.**

1. In a group, discuss why the accident happened. Talk about how DIY could prevent the accident from happening again.

2. Imagine you are the manager. Complete the form using the ideas you discussed in your group.

DIY   **Manager's Investigation Report**

Instructions:
- ✓ Review Employee Accident Report.
- ✓ Interview witnesses.
- ✓ Complete this report.

Name of manager: _____ *NE I* _____

Why did this accident happen?
Be as clear as possible.

Reasons:

1. _The plywood was ten inches over the safety line_
2. _Andy wasn't wearing his hat._
3. _Both employees were careless._
4. _____
5. _____

(Use more space if necessary.)

How can DIY prevent a similar accident from happening again?

Employees should _n't disobey the safety rules._

Employees must _wear their hat all the time_

DIY should _____

DIY must _____

Managers should _n't ask the employees to work so many hours on overtime_

Managers must _keep an eye on what the employees are doing._

Signature of manager completing the form: _____

Date: _____

Expanding the Topic

Connecting Reading with Writing

Choose one of the following writing exercises. Use vocabulary that you've learned in this chapter to make your writing clear and interesting.

1. Have you ever been in a car accident? Have you ever seen a car accident? Write a clear description of the accident. It might help to draw a picture of what happened. Make sure you explain why the accident happened and use the correct sequence, or order of events.

2. Imagine you are an education officer working at the local fire station. One of your responsibilities is to give safety classes to young teenagers who want to work as babysitters. Write a list of do's and don'ts that will help babysitters look after children safely.

3. What should you do if the fire alarm goes off while you are at school? Do you know your escape route? Do you know a safe meeting place? Discuss these questions with other students in your class, and find out about your school's safety plan. Make a flyer for your classroom that clearly explains what you should do in case of fire.

4. Using information and vocabulary that you have learned from Readings 1 and 2, write a paragraph about what you should do if a fire breaks out at your home while you are sleeping. Don't forget to write about how you would help other people in the building. As you write, you will need to use sequence words such as *first, next,* and *after.*

Exploring Online

Complete the activities using the Internet. If you need help with the computer, or have questions about doing an Internet search, ask your teacher or a classmate to help you.

There is a lot of information on the Web about fire safety and general first aid. You can get this information and improve your English at the same time. Of course, if you do have an emergency, are in an accident, or are injured, seek help from professionals immediately.

1. Go online and use a major search engine such as www.google.com or www.yahoo.com to find information about fire safety for children. Print it out and bring it to class to discuss.

2. Do a Web search for "First Aid." You can also go directly to a medical Web site such as www.webmd.com. Find out what you should do if someone has chest pains, if someone has an eye injury, or if someone gets burned. Report to the class on what you learned.

3. If you live in an area that has earthquakes, hurricanes, snowstorms, or flooding, search for information about how to prepare for one of these disasters and what to do in that disaster. Share the information with your class in the form of an oral presentation. Make your presentation more interesting by designing a safety poster or making up a safety quiz.

3

Voting Counts

South Africans waiting to vote. On the day of South Africa's first post-apartheid election, voters stand in long lines outside polling stations waiting to cast their ballots. (Photographed April 27, 1994)

Chapter 3 is about elections and citizenship. Reading 1 describes elections around the world. Next, you will read flyers for a local election. Reading 3 is about becoming a citizen of the United States.

In this chapter, you will practice:

Reading Skills

➡ Previewing a reading

➡ Finding main ideas

➡ Predicting

➡ Distinguishing facts from opinions

Vocabulary Skills

➡ Previewing vocabulary

➡ Using context clues to understand vocabulary

➡ Understanding and using the suffix: *-tion*

Life Skills

➡ Answering citizenship questions

➡ Reading and discussing election flyers

Before You Read

Previewing

Discuss the questions in small groups.

1. Have you ever voted in an election in your native country? What kind of election was it?

2. Who is allowed to vote in your native country? In the country where you live now, how old do you need to be to vote?

3. The title of the reading is "Are All Elections Fair?" How would you answer this question? What makes an election fair?

Previewing Vocabulary

These words are in Reading 1 on pages 58 to 60. Read the words and their definitions. Then choose the best word to complete each sentence. Be sure to change verbs to the correct form.

Word	Definition
declared	stated officially
candidate	a person who wants to be elected to a political position
close race	an election where the candidates have almost the same number of votes
conclude	decide something after thinking carefully about the information
condemn	say very strongly that you do not approve of something
confidential	intended to be kept secret
election	an occasion when you vote in order to choose someone for an official position
the public	all the ordinary people in a country or city
reject	refuse to agree with or accept something
verify	find out if something is correct or true

1. I am going to vote for the _candidate_ who promises to help people pay for health care.

2. The 2000 presidential election between Al Gore and George W. Bush was a _close race_. The two candidates had almost the same number of votes and it took over a month to get final election results.

continued

3. George Bush was ___declared___ the winner of the 2000 election, although Al Gore in fact won more votes.

4. When fighting between two political groups broke out, the government _____ the violence and called for peace.

5. There is a(n) _____ every four years to choose the president of the United States.

6. When the rebel group tried to talk with the government, the president of the country _____ their offer to talk. He said his government would never work with these rebels.

7. The group _____ from their careful two-week study of the results that the election was fair.

8. When the president presented his tax plan to _____, most people supported his ideas.

9. You don't have to tell anyone who you voted for. It is ___confidential___.

10. I have just moved to this city. I need to _____ that I am registered to vote here.

Now Read

Are All Elections Fair? — *эрсил аорса был*

1   If you look up the word *democracy* in a dictionary, you might see this definition: a system of government in which everyone in a country can vote to elect its leaders. The word *democracy* is Greek and means "rule by the people." Elections are an essential part of a democracy. In Ancient Greek times, elections were quite simple. There were clear rules about who could and could not vote, and the number of voters was very small. Today, elections are more complicated. Every election has many rules, and there are millions of people who can vote. It is very important to make sure that elections are fair. This is because only a fair election results in a democratic government. So what do we mean by a fair election, and are all elections fair?

2   An election is fair when several conditions are met. First, a fair and free election begins with several political parties and candidates presenting their ideas to the public. These candidates must be free to argue and disagree with one another and to discuss issues and opinions. People should not be afraid to listen to the issues and

continued

to choose their candidates. Second, voters must be able to vote easily, and the process has to be confidential—no one is allowed to see how a person voted. Finally, all votes should be counted quickly and accurately, and the results must be announced publicly. When these conditions are met, an election is fair and free and results in a democratically formed government.

3   Citizens of some countries, however, worry that their elections may not be fair. When many citizens believe this, the government can ask an international group of experts, called observers, to come and watch the election. This group either verifies that the election is fair or rejects the election as unfair. The observers write detailed reports and make suggestions to improve the voting system for the future. One organization that observes elections is the Carter Center. The Carter Center was started by former United States president Jimmy Carter and his wife, Roslyn. Representatives from the Carter Center have observed over thirty elections around the world since 1989.

4   Sometimes observers decide that an election was not fair, as they did in Zimbabwe in 2002. Observers were concerned about the political violence in Zimbabwe before the election. They worried that ordinary people would be afraid to vote against Zimbabwe's leader of twenty-two years, President Robert Mugabe. The Norwegian Observer Mission carefully monitored the election. They went to many different towns and villages in Zimbabwe and watched people voting. They

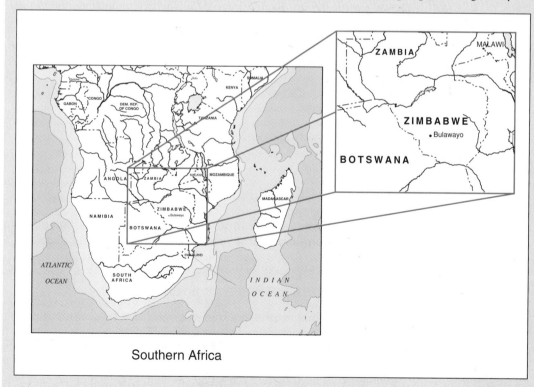

Southern Africa

continued

concluded that the Zimbabwe election of 2002 was not fair. The United States, Britain, and the European Union also condemned the election as unfair. Another observer group led by prime ministers of Australia, South Africa, and Nigeria came to the same conclusion. The government of Robert Mugabe, however, declared that the election was fair.

5   In 2000, the United States also had a serious problem with its presidential election. Many people believed that this election was unfair. It was a very close race between George W. Bush and Al Gore. These two candidates had almost the same number of votes. In the United States, each state has a number of electoral votes. The candidate who wins the majority of individual votes in a state wins these electoral votes. In 2000, it was such a close race that results depended on one state: Florida. Whoever won that state would be the next president of the United States. However, people in Florida complained that they experienced problems when they voted. Some said they voted for the wrong candidate because the ballot was confusing. Others said that many votes were not counted because the voting machines did not work properly. As a result, Florida's Supreme Court[1] ordered election officials to count the votes again. However, the highest court in the country, the U.S. Supreme Court, stopped this recount. George W. Bush was declared the winner. Americans accepted the results, but many argued that the votes in Florida were not correctly counted.

6   Democracy is a complicated form of government, and elections can be equally complicated. Observer organizations, such as the Carter Center and the Norwegian Observer Mission, will no doubt remain busy trying to make sure that elections throughout the world are fair. *rechecked*

[1]**Supreme Court:** the highest court of either a state or a country

After You Read

How Well Did You Read?

Read the statements. Write *T* (true), *F* (false), or *N* (not enough information). Underline the information in the reading that supports your answer.

_____**T**_____ 1. Democracy is an ancient form of government.

_____**F**_____ 2. In a free election, there is no disagreement.

_____**F**_____ 3. The final results in a free election must be confidential.

_____**T**_____ 4. Organizations that observe elections are busier today than they were in the past.

_____**F**_____ 5. Americans agreed that the 2000 presidential election was fair and free.

Check Your Understanding

A. Discuss the questions in small groups. Give clear reasons for your answers.

1. If you have participated in an election, did you think it was fair and free? Explain your answer.

2. Do you think it is a good idea for some countries to invite a group of international observers to monitor elections? Explain your answer.

3. Should all citizens in a country be allowed to vote? What should be the minimum age? What about people in jail? What about people who are citizens, but are not currently living in that country?

B. Read each question and circle the letter of the best answer.

1. What is the main idea of Reading 1?

   a. Many countries have problems with elections because elections are complicated.
   b. Several important conditions are necessary in order for an election to be free and fair.
   c. International observers can verify or reject elections around the world.

2. Which statement is not correct according to paragraph 1?

   a. Elections are a very important part of democracy.
   b. Elections were less complicated in Ancient Greece.
   c. All elections result in a democratically elected government.

3. Why were international observers worried about the Zimbabwe election?

   a. They believed President Mugabe had been in power too long.
   b. They thought voters would not feel free to vote.
   c. They thought people would vote against the government.

4. What is the main idea of paragraph 4?

   a. The Norwegian Observer Mission rejected the Zimbabwe election because they found the election was not fair.
   b. The United States, Britain, and the European Union came to the same conclusion as the Norwegians, and Mugabe's government agreed.
   c. Although Mugabe's government argued the election was fair, various international observers condemned the election as unfair.

5. Why do you think the Florida Supreme Court ordered a recount of votes in the Bush–Gore presidential election?

   a. The U.S. Supreme Court ordered a recount.
   b. The Florida Supreme Court wanted one candidate to win, and it was a close race.
   c. There were complaints about the voting process, and it was a close race.

continued

C. Imagine you are a member of an international team of observers, and you are observing an election. Read the five descriptions of situations. Using the information you learned from Reading 1, decide if each situation is an example of a free and fair election, or an unfair practice. Share your answers with a partner. Give clear reasons for your decisions.

1. You are in a village where many elderly people cannot read and write. One elderly man is trying to vote, but he cannot read the names on the ballot. A government official holds the ballot for him and kindly reads the names. The elderly man tells the official who he wants to vote for. The official marks a name and drops the vote in the box.

   Free and fair? _____   Unfair? _____

   Reasons: _____

   _____

2. You are in a busy city where many of the voters speak different languages. The official language of the country is English, but a lot of people don't speak it. You are reading a ballot before an election to make sure the ballot is fair. You see the instructions are printed in several languages. Next to each candidate's name is a photograph. Voters put a check next to the photograph of the candidate they want to elect.

   Free and fair? _____   Unfair? _____

   Reasons: _____

   _____

3. You are at a voting station in a small farming village. Government soldiers surround the station. They are carrying guns and silently watching all the voters. There is a long line of people waiting to vote. A large sign says the voting station will close at 8:00 P.M. At 8:00 the officials close the station. Many people are still waiting. They try to explain they have been waiting for hours. The soldiers move closer. The people go home.

   Free and fair? _____   Unfair? _____

   Reasons: _____

   _____

4. You are in a modern, well-organized voting station. You hear a person arguing with a voting official. This woman has recently moved to the city. She forgot to change her voting address. The official explains she cannot vote because she is not on the list. The woman takes out her driver's license and asks if she can vote. She is angry when the official says *no*. She says she has the right to vote.

Free and fair? _____   Unfair? _____

Reasons: _____

_____

5. You are in a country during a national election. The choice for voters is to choose the current president for another five years or reject the president. There is no candidate running against the current president. Voting is confidential, and the government promises to count every vote—including the *no* votes.

Free and fair? _____   Unfair? _____

Reasons: _____

_____

Finding Main Ideas

Read the paragraphs about different kinds of elections. What is the main idea of each paragraph? Answer these questions about each paragraph to find the main idea:

What is the topic?
What does the writer say about the topic?

Write the main idea on the line. Then compare your answers with a partner's.

1.   In many countries children learn about voting at a very early age. At schools, children vote for a class captain or president. They vote for the leader of a game or who will be on a team. Through this process, children learn responsibility. They learn that they can make a difference by voting. These early election experiences prepare them for participating in elections as adults.

Main idea: _____

2.   Sometimes people feel that only important political leaders can make a difference. This, however, is not always true. Ordinary people can make a huge difference. When Janet Chung, for example, found her local library had to close because of lack of funding, she decided to do something about it. First, she called a neighborhood meeting and explained the problem. She asked people to vote whether or not to save the library. The vote was unanimous—everyone wanted to keep their library. Next, Janet made flyers about the library and sent them to all her friends and neighbors. Then, she wrote a letter about saving the library and 500 people signed it. Janet sent this letter to her elected

continued

representative. He quickly realized this was an important issue, and he promised to fight for the library. He kept his promise, and the library was saved. This shows that an ordinary person can make a real difference.

Main idea: _____

3.   World War I changed the life of women in Britain in many ways. My great-grandmother, Claire, grew up in a small, industrial town in the north of England. When I was young, she would tell me stories about the war, which started when she was sixteen. Many young men left the town and joined the army. Claire wanted to do something to help, so she joined a group of young women who went to work in a local factory that made army uniforms. She also learned to drive trucks. This was a new experience for women at this time. Before the war, very few women worked—especially in dirty factories where the work was hard and sometimes dangerous. They were not allowed to vote in elections. Women were supposed to stay at home and take care of their families. When the war finally ended, women demanded the right to vote. They argued they had shown they were equal to men by helping in the war effort. In 1918, women gained that right, and Claire proudly voted for the first time. She never missed an opportunity to vote after that, and neither have I.

Main idea: _____

Reading 2   *Part A: It's Time to Change!*

Before You Read

Discuss these questions in small groups.

1. Would you like to be a politician? Why or why not?

2. What kind of person makes a good politician?

3. How do people become politicians?

Using Context Clues to Understand Vocabulary

The words in bold print are in Reading 2, Part A, on pages 66 and 67. Use context clues and circle the letter of the answer closest in meaning to the word in bold print.

1. During an election, people vote for their **representative** in the local or state government. The person who receives the most votes is the winner.

   a. a person who is chosen to act or speak for someone else
   b. a leader of a political party
   c. a person who works for the government

2. Scientists are warning us that we must protect the **environment.** If we don't, life on Earth will suffer.

    a. government
    b. air, land, and water
    c. oceans and rivers

3. In the early twentieth century, the Australian government wanted people to move to Australia. They offered cheap land and free travel to **encourage** people to move there.

    a. make someone feel bad
    b. make a person feel healthy
    c. make someone more likely to do something

4. There are many **advantages** to living in a big city: good restaurants, exciting night life, interesting museums, and wonderful theaters.

    a. types of entertainment
    b. good qualities
    c. problems

5. This city is growing too quickly and this causes many problems. We need to **restrict** the number of new homes until problems, like traffic and crowded schools, are solved.

    a. limit
    b. increase
    c. vote on

6. Unfortunately, many countries still burn fossil fuels, such as wood and coal, that **pollute** the air.

    a. destroy something
    b. make dangerously dirty
    c. create smoke

7. The city center was old and many buildings were falling down. The government decided to **restore** the old buildings and turn them into tourist attractions.

    a. paint and clean
    b. change something back to the way it was
    c. take down

8. After the Chernobyl nuclear accident, many Ukrainian parents moved away from the area because they wanted to **raise** their families in a safe environment.

    a. increase in number
    b. move to a safe place
    c. take care of until grown

It's time to vote for a state representative in Silverlake, a small but growing town in central California. Tom Edwin and Susan Ferguson both want to be the next representative. Only one person will win the election. Both candidates want the public to know their ideas and opinions. They have written flyers about themselves, and they will give the flyers to people all over the town. The first flyer tells what Tom Edwin thinks about the city of Silverlake.

It's Time to Change!

1   I'd like to introduce myself. My name is Tom Edwin. My family has lived in this city for generations. In fact, my great-great-grandfather came here from Iowa by horse and wagon in the late 1850s. It was a long, hard journey, and the Edwin family has been here ever since. My family has always believed in helping people. My grandfather was elected as state representative, and his son—my father—was elected as city mayor. Now it's my turn. Now, more than any other time, I believe this city needs strong leadership. With your vote, I will be proud to become the next state representative for

2   Silverlake, and I will provide that leadership.

3   *Why do I say this city needs leadership?*

Look around you. Look at the rivers full of dying fish. When I was a boy, I used to catch fish, and we'd eat them for dinner. Now I don't allow my children near the water. Look at the land. How many of you remember the fields and woods full of deer, raccoons, and even bears? Can you remember how green it all was? Corn grew higher than your Dad's shoulders. Apricots and peaches were as round and yellow as the sun. And now what do you see? Fields and woods? No! You see only ugly concrete and steel buildings. The beautiful land has disappeared.

4   Silverlake used to be a wonderful town to raise a family in. It was peaceful here. It was a small town, and neighbors knew each other. The schools were good, and when our children graduated, there were jobs for them right here in town. Families stayed together. When the kids got sick, the town clinic was always ready to see them. And you know what? The streets were safe. My family never locked our doors at night because we didn't need to. Yes, this was a good place to raise your kids.

5   *Today life in Silverlake is very different. Let's look at the problems.*

- In the last ten years our population has quadrupled. Yes, it has grown by 400%! Silverlake has grown too quickly, and now we have problems.
- The traffic is terrible. Our schools are overcrowded.
- In the past, our state representatives saw the money that new industry could bring to town. They offered low taxes and cheap land to encourage large businesses to settle here.

continued

- New businesses came to Silverlake, but these industries destroyed the environment. Our political leaders turned away while this was happening.
- Silverlake grew without planning. Now it's time to start planning.

6 *With careful planning, we can enjoy the advantages of industry and restore this city to the beautiful place it once was. How do we do this?*

- Of course the businesses must stay. However, we must restrict future growth and not allow so many new businesses to move to this area.
- Factories must pay to clean up our rivers. We cannot allow them to pump their toxic waste into the water and the soil. They must stop polluting our environment.

*I am asking for your vote. Together, we can restore Silverlake. We can have it all—
new neighbors, jobs, a good life, and a beautiful city.
We can make Silverlake the place it used to be . . . only better!*

VOTE FOR TOM EDWIN!

After You Read

How Well Did You Read?

Read the statements. Write *T* (true), *F* (false), or *N* (not enough information).
Underline the information in the reading that supports your answer.

_____ 1. Tom's family has a long history in Silverlake.

_____ 2. Tom is the first member of his family to be involved in politics.

_____ 3. Tom believes Silverlake today is better than it was in the past.

_____ 4. Tom is worried about the environment.

_____ 5. Tom will win this election.

Check Your Understanding

A. Discuss the questions in small groups. Then share your ideas with the class.

1. Tom describes Silverlake of the past and Silverlake of the present. Which do you think sounds like the better place to live? Why?

2. Sometimes when we think about the past, we remember the good things and forget the bad things. Do you think Tom has forgotten some of the bad things about the past? What kinds of things might Tom have forgotten?

3. Do you think Tom's ideas about solving the pollution problems in Silverlake are good? What other suggestions do you have to improve the environment?

continued

B. Answer the questions in complete sentences. Use your own words.

1. What is the main idea of Tom's flyer?

   _____

2. Why does Tom talk about his family in the first paragraph?

   _____

3. Why does Tom believe Silverlake needs a strong leader?

   _____

4. Why does Tom talk about the animals, the fruit, and the vegetables in paragraph 3?

   _____

5. Tom states that political leaders encouraged new businesses to settle in Silverlake. Why do you think these leaders wanted new businesses to come to town?

   _____

6. *New businesses came to Silverlake, but these industries destroyed the environment. Our political leaders **turned away** while this was happening.* What does **turned away** mean?

   _____

7. Tom also states that the new businesses polluted the environment. How do you think a factory or business might pollute the environment?

   _____

8. In paragraph 6, Tom argues that the residents can enjoy the "advantages of industry." What advantages, or good things, could industrial development bring to a town?

   _____

Before You Read

Previewing Vocabulary

These words are in Reading 2, Part B, on page 70. Read the words and their definitions. Then choose the best word to complete each sentence. Be sure to change verbs to the correct form.

Word	Definition
better off	have more money than before, or more than other people
designated	chosen for a special purpose
dynamic	interesting, exciting, full of energy
incentive	something that encourages someone to work harder or move to an area
quality of life	how good or bad one's life is
revenue	money that is earned by a company or that the government receives from taxes
thrive	become successful, strong, or healthy
treatments	ways to try to cure sickness or an injury
zone	part of an area that has a special purpose

1. You cannot build a commercial building in a housing _____.

2. Computer companies _____ because everyone wants the latest technology.

3. A company like Nintendo makes billions of dollars in _____ each year.

4. John offered his son $5.00 as a(n) _____ to improve his grades.

5. Although the _____ is generally better today for many people, it continues to be very hard for others.

6. Doctors are trying to find new and better _____ for cancer and many other serious illnesses.

7. Some people love the city because it is a _____ place. Others prefer small towns with a slower pace.

8. Parents were angry because the city _____ an area next to a school as the site for a new prison.

9. Skilled workers are generally _____ than unskilled workers because they are paid higher wages.

Next you will read a flyer written by the second candidate, Susan Ferguson. Compare the title of Susan's flyer with the title of Tom Edwin's flyer. Do you think the candidates are going to have similar ideas or different ideas?

The Future Is Bright!

1   This town has grown up quickly. Over the last ten years, it has changed from a quiet, sleepy little community to a dynamic city. Change is always hard. There are always some folks who don't want to change. They are afraid of the future. Today, some of these folks are crying "Let's stop the progress! Let's go back to the past!" However, if we look carefully at life today compared to life ten years ago, we'll see that we are much better off today.

2   What was Silverlake like ten years ago? It is true that the river was a lot cleaner. It is also true that there were more woods and fields. Ten years ago, there were farmers here. But what was life like in Silverlake ten years ago? Silverlake was beautiful, but life was hard. We had one hospital, and if you were hurt badly, you had to travel fifty miles for treatment. The schools were old. The students in Mr. Perkins's biology class always knew when it was raining. They got wet because the roof leaked right onto their heads. The roads were terrible. Life was hard. No wonder our kids were leaving Silverlake.

3   What is life like today in this city of ours? We have some work to do, but our lives today are much better than ten years ago. We've grown fast, and we have some problems. Cleaning the river is a top priority. We could also improve some of the industrial areas. But look at the good things we have today:

- *More people are employed today than at any other time in Silverlake's history.*
- *The quality of life is better today.*
- *Our schools are modern, with state-of-the-art technology.*
- *The community college offers degrees and training in a wide variety of subjects.*
- *Our hospital wins awards for its research.*
- *Our streets are busy, the stores are thriving, the theaters are full, and the restaurants are serving up wonderful menus!*
- *Life is definitely better today.*

4   Environmental cleanup is expensive. How are we going to do this? We need to increase revenue, so here's what I propose:

- *Lower business taxes to encourage more companies to come to Silverlake.*
- *Offer additional incentives, such as low-interest loans, to attract new businesses.*
- *Write environmental guidelines for factories.*
- *Designate areas as industrial zones, and plan these zones carefully.*

If you elect me, I will clean up this city. But I will not take us back to the past. Together, we have a great future here in Silverlake.

VOTE FOR SUSAN FERGUSON!

After You Read

How Well Did You Read?

Read the statements. Write *A* if you think Susan would agree or *D* if you think she would disagree.

_____ 1. Some people are worried about change.

_____ 2. The city must increase business taxes to pay for the environmental cleanup.

_____ 3. Silverlake was better off in the past.

_____ 4. Silverlake was a beautiful place in the past, but life was not easy for residents.

_____ 5. Silverlake doesn't need more businesses.

Check Your Understanding

A. Work in small groups. Discuss the questions, and share your answers with the class.

1. What are the main differences between Susan's ideas and Tom's ideas?

2. Do the two candidates agree on anything?

3. Who would you vote for? Why?

B. Read each question and circle the letter of the best answer.

1. What is the main idea of Reading 2, Part B?

   a. People had a better life in the past than they do today.
   b. Although there are problems today in Silverlake, life is better than it used to be.
   c. The quality of life is very good today.

2. Why does Susan describe Silverlake ten years ago?

   a. To describe the high quality of life
   b. To argue that people who believe the past is better than the present are wrong
   c. To say that the natural environment was a lot cleaner than it is now

3. In paragraph 3, Susan states that *"Cleaning the river is a top priority."* This means _____.

   a. Silverlake needs to solve other problems before it cleans the river
   b. cleaning the river is not important at all
   c. cleaning the river is the first thing that needs to be done in Silverlake

4. In paragraph 4, Susan argues that _____.

   a. businesses must pay higher taxes to clean up the environment
   b. Silverlake should lower business taxes to encourage more companies to come
   c. Silverlake needs to restrict new businesses

Distinguishing Facts from Opinions

Good readers know how to distinguish, or separate, facts from opinions. A **fact** is a known truth; an **opinion** is an idea or a belief about something. Facts do not change, but one person's opinion might be very different from another person's opinion. You cannot agree or disagree with a fact, but you can agree or disagree with an opinion.

How do you recognize opinions?

- Opinions are often introduced by phrases such as *In my opinion,* or *I think,* or *I believe.*
- Adjectives can express opinions. *That movie was terrible* or *Learning English is hard.*
- Sometimes opinions are expressed with adjectives or adverbs in the comparative or superlative form. For example, *This book is better than that book* or *This is the best dictionary.*

A. Work with a partner. Tom Edwin and Susan Ferguson both use facts and opinions to persuade the voters. Discuss which of the following statements from the flyers are facts and which are opinions. Write *Fact* or *Opinion* next to each sentence.

1. _____ My grandfather was elected as state representative, and his son—my father—was elected as city mayor.

2. _____ When I was a boy, I used to catch fish, and we'd eat them for dinner.

3. _____ Silverlake used to be a wonderful town to raise a family in.

4. _____ In the last ten years our population has quadrupled.

5. _____ Now, more than any other time, I believe this city needs strong leadership.

6. _____ We had one hospital, and if you were hurt badly, you had to travel fifty miles for treatment.

7. _____ The quality of life is better today.

8. _____ Silverlake was beautiful, but life was hard.

9. _____ The community college offers degrees and training in a wide variety of subjects.

10. _____ Our hospital wins awards for its research.

B. Now it is your turn to write your opinions about the candidates. Write five sentences about the two candidates. Use words from the skill box on page 72 to show you are expressing an opinion.

1. _____

2. _____

3. _____

4. _____

5. _____

A Question of Citizenship

Before You Read

The previous readings in this chapter are about elections. In order to vote in an election, you must be a citizen of the country where the election is taking place. Reading 3 on pages 74 and 75 is about how to become a citizen of the United States.

Previewing

Look at the chart. Discuss these questions with a partner.

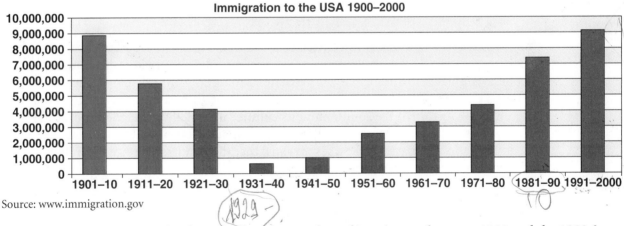

Immigration to the USA 1900–2000

Source: www.immigration.gov

1. What happened to the number of immigrants between 1910 and the 1950s? Why do you think this happened?

2. How many immigrants arrived between 1981 and 1990? How many more arrived in the next ten years?

3. Which countries do you think most immigrants came from between 1970 and 2000?

4. Why do think immigrants come to the United States?

5. Do you think the number of immigrants arriving between 2000 and 2010 will increase, decrease, or stay the same? Explain your answer.

A Question of Citizenship

1   America is built on immigration. In fact, according to the Bureau of Citizenship and Immigration Services (BCIS), 66,089,431 people immigrated to the United States between 1820 and 2000. In the year 2000, a total of 849,807 people immigrated to America. Today, thousands of people from all over the world continue to come to the United States. They come from countries as far apart as Ethiopia and Ukraine, China and Mexico. They speak different languages, and they have different customs. Although they come for different reasons, which include war, poverty, new opportunities, family, and religion, these immigrants have a lot in common. They want to start a new life, but they understand that this life will be full of challenges. One of these challenges is becoming a citizen.

2   Most people in the world are citizens by birth. In other words, they were either born in their country or born of citizen parents. A child who is born in a country will be a citizen of that country even if his or her parents are not citizens. Likewise, when a child is born to, for example, German parents, the child is a citizen of Germany whether or not the parents are living in Germany. Most countries follow these basic guidelines. This sometimes results in a person having two nationalities, which is called dual citizenship. Some countries allow their citizens to keep dual citizenship, while others ask them to choose one nationality when they become adults.

3   Another way to become a citizen of a country is through a legal process called naturalization. Different countries have different rules about naturalization. In most countries, including the United States, immigrants must live in that country for a number of years, speak the language well enough to communicate, know about the history of the country and its culture, and finally, be of good moral character. This means they cannot have a criminal background. In America, immigrants also have to take a test to show that they understand American history and the American system of government.

4   Applicants who speak English as a second language are often very worried about this test. They worry about their English and their knowledge of history and politics. They also know that when they feel nervous, it is more difficult to speak English. Many schools, community centers, libraries, and colleges understand this, and offer classes to help prepare people for the test.

continued

5   What is this test that scares so many people? Is it long? Is it difficult? In fact, the test often only takes about ten minutes. The BCIS interviewers usually ask about 12 questions from a list of 100 questions. Sample questions are readily available on a variety of Web sites for applicants to practice before the test. The applicants can make one or two mistakes but must get most of the questions correct. Since hundreds of thousands of people become citizens each year, obviously the majority of applicants prepare very well.

6   How would you do on this test? Would it make you nervous? These questions are samples provided by the BCIS. More questions can be found on the BCIS Web site at www.immigration.gov.

1. What are the colors of the flag?

2. What is the 4th of July?

3. Who was the first president of the United States?

4. Who is the vice president of the United States today?

5. For how long do we elect a president?

6. What is the Constitution?

7. What are the duties of the Supreme Court?

8. Who was Martin Luther King Jr.?

9. Which president ended slavery?

10. Name one right guaranteed by the First Amendment.

After You Read

How Well Did You Read?

Work with a partner. Read the statements. Write *T* (true), *F* (false), or *N* (not enough information). Underline the information in the reading that supports your answer.

___F___ 1. Immigrants come to the United States for many different reasons and do not have a lot in common.

___F___ 2. More people throughout the world become citizens by naturalization than by birth.

We don't know 3. All countries require a test for citizenship.

___F___ 4. In the United States, people have the choice to take the citizenship test in their first language or in English.

___F___ 5. Applicants taking the citizenship test in the United States need to know the capital cities of all fifty states.

Check Your Understanding

Work with a partner. Circle the letter of the best answer.

1. What is the main idea of the reading?

   a. More than sixty-six million people have come to live in the United States since 1820.
   b. One of the most important challenges for immigrants is to become a citizen.
   c. America is a nation built on immigration.

2. According to paragraph 2, if a child is born in Germany to non-German parents, what is true?

   a. The child will not be a German citizen.
   b. The child will need to take a test to become a citizen.
   c. The child will be a German citizen by birth.

3. *Immigrants must . . . be of good moral character* (paragraph 3). What does this mean?

   a. The person wanting citizenship should be a kind person.
   b. The person wanting citizenship should be able to speak English.
   c. The person wanting citizenship should not have committed any crimes.

4. Why do applicants who speak English as a second language worry about the United States citizenship test?

   a. They want to take it in their own language.
   b. They worry that they will not understand the questions.
   c. They haven't practiced the sample questions.

5. Which of the following statements contains an opinion?

    a. Another way to become a citizen is through a legal process called naturalization.

    b. Once a person has lived in America for several years, he or she can apply to become a citizen.

    c. It would be better if applicants could take the test in their native language.

6. Which sentence means the same as the following?

    Some countries allow their citizens to keep dual citizenship, while others ask them to choose one nationality when they become adults.

    a. Some countries ask people to choose one nationality when they become adults; other countries permit dual citizenship.

    b. Some countries do not allow dual citizenship.

    c. Some countries allow dual citizenship; however, all countries ask people to choose one nationality when they become adults.

7. Why do thousands of immigrants pass the citizenship test, according to the reading?

    a. There are a lot of Web sites with practice questions.

    b. The test is very easy.

    c. People prepare carefully for the test.

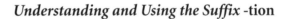

Vocabulary Skill	*Understanding and Using the Suffix* -tion
	In Chapter 2 you learned the suffixes *-ful* and *-less*. Another very common suffix is *-tion*. This suffix changes a verb to a noun, for example, *elect* → *election*.

A. Work in small groups. Read the list and discuss the meaning of the words. Check your dictionary if you don't know a word.

Verb	Noun
1. act	action
2. apply	application
3. celebrate	celebration
4. elect	election
5. inform	information
6. instruct	instruction
7. invent	invention
8. invite	invitation
9. protect	protection
10. suggest	suggestion

B. Complete the sentences with words from the list in Part A. Pay attention to whether the sentence requires a noun or a verb. Be sure to use the correct verb form and check if the noun should be singular or plural.

1. The teacher _____instructed_____ the students to complete the test. Her _____instructions_____ were very clear.

2. My friend decided to _____ her twenty-first birthday with a huge party. She invited fifty friends and even had fireworks for the _____.

3. Sunscreen _____ the skin from the harmful rays of the sun. Children especially need this _____ from the sun.

4. Three months ago, I decided to _____ for U.S. citizenship. I completed the _____ and sent it to the BCIS.

5. One student in the class _____ that the teacher should not give homework because it was summer and students should have time to relax. The teacher, however, did not follow his _____.

6. In the recent state _____, the Democrats won a majority in the House. However, James Moore, a Republican, was _____ governor.

7. It's not enough to think about being kind. Remember the saying, "_____ speak louder than words." You should _____ in a kind way toward other people.

8. Benjamin Franklin loved to think of new ways of doing things. He loved to _____ things. One of his most famous _____ was the lightening rod. It protected a house from lightening.

9. In elementary schools, teachers usually don't like children to hand out birthday party _____ in class. Children who are not _____ can feel hurt.

10. I read the _____ from the BCIS carefully and completed the application for a passport. One month later, the BCIS _____ me to send a photograph.

Expanding the Topic

Connecting Reading with Writing

Choose one of the following writing exercises. Use vocabulary that you've learned in this chapter to make your writing clear and interesting.

1. Choose a country other than the United States. How do people in this country select their government?

2. In Reading 3, the author stated that many people feel nervous about taking the citizenship test, and that when they feel nervous, they forget their English. Do you feel nervous when you take a test? Do you forget your English? Write a paragraph about how you feel when you take a test. Include examples to make your writing clear and interesting.

3. Choose another country. How do people become a citizen of this country? Is the process similar to or different from the U.S. process?

4. Why did the students in your class come to this country? Interview your classmates to find the reasons, and then write a paragraph beginning with the topic sentence:

   There are several reasons why my classmates came to this country.

5. It's election time! The Student Organization at your school needs a new student president. You want to be the next president, so you write a flyer to persuade your fellow students to vote for you. Your flyer should include some problems you think need to be fixed and some good ideas you have to improve the organization. Include both facts and opinions.

Exploring Online

Complete the activities using the Internet. If you need help with the computer, or have questions about doing an Internet search, ask your teacher or a classmate to help you.

1. Use one of the major search engines to research "citizenship." Find a site that has sample citizenship questions. How many of the questions can you answer? Download the questions, and bring them to class with you. Practice asking each other the questions in groups. Download the answers, too. You may need them!

2. Reading 3 cites statistics, or numbers, provided on the BCIS Web site. Using statistics adds more detail to writing. The Internet is a powerful and convenient tool to use when searching for statistics. Use a search engine and type in either "Statistical Year Book" or "BCIS." You will find a lot of information about immigration. Find a site that shows the number of people who came to live in the United States from different countries in a given year. Using information from that site, complete the following table:

Year: _____

Name of Country	Numbers of Immigrants

Source: www. _____

3. How do you register to vote in the country where you now live? Do an Internet search for information about how to register to vote. Try the search words "voter registration." Find a registration form. Print out one copy of the form and bring it to class. Be prepared to tell your class what kind of information is needed to complete the registration form.

Leaders of Yesterday

Chapter 4 includes readings about well-known leaders from different parts of the world. The first reading is a brief biography of King Hussein of Jordan. In Reading 2, you will read about Indira Gandhi. Reading 3 is about Nelson Mandela.

In this chapter, you will practice:

Reading Skills

- → Previewing a reading
- → Identifying supporting details
- → Identifying and using time phrases
- → Distinguishing facts from opinions
- → Recognizing time clauses
- → Paraphrasing
- → Highlighting

Vocabulary Skills

- → Using context clues to understand vocabulary

Life Skills

- → Keeping up on current events
- → Searching for information on the Internet

King Hussein of Jordan

Before You Read

Sharing Previous Knowledge

Discuss the questions with a partner. When you have finished, share your information with the class. Use this information to complete the chart that follows.

1. How many of the political leaders on page 81 do you recognize?

2. Which country did each leader govern or rule? When did they govern?

3. What else do you know about them?

Name of Leader	Country	Facts About the Leader

Previewing

To preview a reading you should:

- look at the title, headings, and illustrations to get the general idea of the reading.
- think about what you already know about the topic.
- predict what will be in the reading.

Answer the questions with a partner.

1. What do you know about King Hussein? (Use the photos, map, and chart on pages 81, 82, and 85 to help you.)

2. How do you think this story about his life will be organized?

Using Context Clues to Understand Vocabulary

The words in bold print are in Reading 1 on page 84. Use context clues and circle the letter of the answer closest in meaning to the word(s) in bold print.

1. America became **independent from** Britain in 1781 after the Revolutionary War. From this time on, Britain no longer governed America.

    a. strong and confident
    b. not controlled by
    c. connected to

2. People all over the world **respected** Mohandas Gandhi for his belief in nonviolent protest. Even today, children all over the world learn about this beloved leader.

    a. admired
    b. were frustrated by
    c. disliked

3. The world was shocked when Anwar Sadat, the president of Egypt, was **assassinated** by soldiers of his own army. Many people were very sad when he died.

    a. not liked
    b. murdered
    c. injured

4. Many people tried to murder King Hussein, but he **survived** and lived a long life.

    a. continued to live
    b. was injured
    c. ignored

5. England has a prime minister and a **monarch.** Both leaders are important, but the prime minister has more political power than the queen.

    a. leader of a country
    b. king or queen
    c. leader of a political party

6. When the Gulf War **broke out** in 1990, many people were worried the war would spread across the Middle East.

    a. began
    b. ended
    c. concluded

7. During the Gulf War, America organized a **coalition** to fight for Kuwait's independence.

    a. one country
    b. the world
    c. a group of countries

continued

8. In the last year of his reign, Hussein met with an enemy he could not **defeat:** cancer.

   a. try to fight against
   b. understand and learn from
   c. win against; overcome

9. King Hussein is remembered as a **moderate** leader who tried to listen to different opinions and to work with all the groups in the Middle East.

   a. reasonable, not extreme
   b. stubborn but smart
   c. dangerous and extreme

Now Read

King Hussein of Jordan

1   King Hussein of Jordan was born on November 14, 1935 in Amman. At that time, Jordan was under British rule. However, in 1946, Jordan became independent, and Abdullah ibn Hussein, Hussein's grandfather, became king. He ruled from 1946 to 1951. As a member of the royal family and Abdullah's favorite grandson, Hussein was encouraged to study hard. He went to schools in Jordan, Egypt, and Great Britain. On July 20, 1951, he learned how dangerous politics could be. He went with his grandfather to the al-Aqsa Mosque in Jerusalem. As they walked into the mosque to pray, an assassin shot and killed his grandfather. The assassin also tried to shoot Hussein, but missed. Some report that a bullet hit and bounced off a medal Hussein was wearing on his chest. This was the first of many violent experiences in the life of this man who became one of the most well-known and respected world leaders of the late twentieth century.

2   In spite of numerous attempts on his life, Hussein became the longest-ruling monarch in this part of the world. He became king in 1953 at the age of seventeen when his father had to give up the throne because of illness. Ruling for the next forty-seven years, Hussein faced danger time and time again. During these years, he survived at least seventeen attempts on his life. His enemies shot at his house and his plane. They poisoned his food and even put acid in his nose drops. Hussein survived all of these attempts.

3   Hussein was known and respected by many nations as a peacemaker in an area of the world that has not enjoyed peace for a long time. He was known as a moderate leader who tried to lead his country through the complex and often violent politics of the Palestinians, the Iraqis, the Israelis, and the Western world. When the first Gulf War broke out in 1990, for example, Hussein took a middle

continued

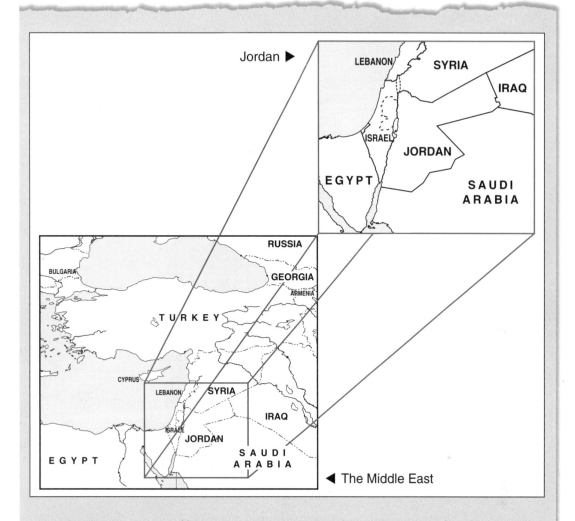

Jordan ▶

◀ The Middle East

path. Because many of his countrymen supported Iraq, Hussein refused to join the coalition of countries against Iraq. At the same time, he made it clear to the coalition that he would work hard to bring a peaceful end to this war. In 1994, he signed a peace agreement with the Israeli prime minister, Yitzhak Rabin. The following year his friend, Prime Minister Rabin, was assassinated.

4   In the last year of his reign, Hussein met with an enemy he could not defeat: cancer. He chose his eldest son, Abdullah, to succeed him. Even when he was weak because of chemotherapy treatments, he left his hospital bed and flew to the Israeli–Palestinian peace talks at Camp David in Maryland. As the dying king explained, "If I had an ounce of strength, I would have done my utmost to be there, and to help in any way I can."[1] A few weeks later, he died, and the world lost a leader who had worked all his life to bring peace to the Middle East.

[1] *Time* Magazine, February 15, 1999, p. 32.

After You Read

How Well Did You Read?

Work with a partner to answer these questions.

1. What two events happened in 1946? _____

_____

2. How did Hussein's grandfather die? _____

3. How did Hussein become king? _____

4. What was one problem Hussein faced as king? _____

Check Your Understanding

Read the questions and circle the letter of the best answers.

1. Hussein became king _____.

   a. immediately after his grandfather was killed
   b. just before Jordan became independent
   c. when his father became too ill to rule

2. How did King Hussein take a middle path in the Gulf War?

   a. He refused to join the coalition and fought with Iraq.
   b. He refused to join the coalition, but tried to end the war peacefully.
   c. He joined with the coalition and tried to end the war peacefully.

3. When did Prime Minister Rabin die?

   a. He died at the beginning of the Gulf War.
   b. He died one year after he signed a peace agreement with King Hussein.
   c. He died in the last year of King Hussein's reign.

4. Why did King Hussein fly to Camp David, Maryland, in 1999 when he was dying from cancer?

   a. He needed chemotherapy.
   b. He chose his son to succeed him.
   c. He wanted to try to help bring peace between the Israelis and Palestinians.

5. King Hussein is known as a peacemaker _____.

   a. because he fought against Iraq in the first Gulf War
   b. because he joined the coalition against Iraq in 1990
   c. because he tried to bring together the different cultures and religions in the Middle East

Reading Skill

Identifying Supporting Details

In Chapter 2 you learned that each paragraph usually has a main idea sentence. The other sentences in the paragraph give **supporting details.** They either explain or give examples that support the main idea.

Example:

Main idea: *In spite of numerous attempts on his life, Hussein became the longest-ruling monarch in this part of the world.*

Supporting details: He became king in 1953 at the age of seventeen.
He ruled for forty-seven years.
During these years, he survived at least seventeen attempts on his life.

Find the main ideas and supporting details for the paragraphs from Reading 1.

1. Paragraph 3

   Main idea: <u>Hussein was known as a peacemaker in a very violent part of the world.</u>

   Supporting details: **a.** He refused to fight in the Gulf War.

   b. _____

   c. _____

2. Paragraph 4

   Main idea: _____

   Supporting details: **a.** _____

   b. _____

   c. _____

Identifying and Using Time Phrases

When you read a biography about a person's life, you need to understand when important events happened. Writers use **time phrases** to show when something happened. Here are some examples of time phrases:

- **In** 1999,
- **On** November 5, 1999,
- **In** May, 1999,
- **From** 1870 **to** 1877,

- **During** this period,
- Three years **later**,
- The **next** year,
- The **previous** year,

When you read an article that is organized chronologically (in time order), pay attention to time phrases.

A. Reread the article on King Hussein. Underline all the time phrases. Then compare your work with a partner's.

B. Read this paragraph about another world leader, Mikhail Gorbachev. He was the last president of the Soviet Union before it divided into independent countries. Complete the time phrases with words from the box.

in	on	from	to	during	later	next	previous

Mikhail Gorbachev was born _____ March 2, 1931.

                           1

_____ his teenage years, he worked for a farm machinery station

     2
that was run by the government. He was bright and ambitious, and

_____ 1952 _____ 1955, he studied law at Moscow

     3   4
State University. _____ 1953, Khrushchev succeeded Stalin as the

               5
Soviet leader, and a new period began in the history of this country.

_____ that year, Gorbachev married Raisa Maximovna.

     6

_____ 1956 _____ 1985, Gorbachev became

     7   8
increasingly involved with politics. _____ these years, he gained

                       9
more and more responsibility and respect as a young political leader. Finally his

hard work paid off because _____ March 1985, he became the Soviet

             10
leader. However, six years _____, Gorbachev resigned as the Soviet

             11
Union fell apart, and individual states like Ukraine declared independence.

Before You Read

Using Context Clues to Understand Vocabulary

The words in bold print are in Reading 2 on pages 90 and 91. Use context clues to guess the meaning of these words. Write the meanings in your own words. Compare your answers with a partner's.

1. Many leaders have several **bodyguards** to protect them from danger.

   bodyguards: _____

2. The Botswana government has improved **agriculture** throughout the country by educating farmers in new and more efficient farming methods.

   agriculture: _____

3. In some parts of the world, people still cook using wood fires. This causes pollution. Governments need to help people **modernize** their cooking methods by providing gas or electric stoves, which are better for the environment.

   modernize: _____

4. International observers decided the election was not fair because the government **limited** the number of people who could vote. Many people were not allowed to vote.

   limited: _____

5. Farmers growing tobacco used to be very **well-off.** Now, however, they are becoming poor because the demand for tobacco has fallen.

   well-off: _____

6. Martin Luther King led many peaceful **protests** against unfair treatment of African Americans. Since thousands took part in these protests, it is remarkable that no one was hurt.

   protests: _____

7. **Industrial** areas of the country are overcrowded because people leave the countryside and move to these areas to look for work in the factories.

   industrial: _____

8. In the 1980s, Ethiopia and Somalia suffered a terrible **drought.** Because the land was too dry to grow anything, many people died.

   drought: _____

Now Read

Indira Gandhi

1   The morning of October 31, 1984, began like most mornings for Indira Gandhi, prime minister of India, the world's largest democracy. After she had breakfast, Indira walked through the garden that connected her home to her office. She was thinking about the busy day ahead. As her two trusted bodyguards approached her, she looked up. The bodyguards took the guns that were supposed to protect her and shot her. Indira Gandhi died instantly.

2   It was a long and often difficult journey to this violent end. The journey began with an unusual childhood. Indira was born into the Nehru family in 1917. At this time, India was ruled by Great Britain. The Nehru family was wealthy and well-known in the city where they lived. When Indira was a very young child, Mohandas Gandhi visited her home and talked to her parents about the need for independence from the British. Mohandas Gandhi became a close family friend, and the Nehru family agreed that India should be independent. As a young girl, Indira met many leading Indian politicians and listened to them discussing politics in her family living room. Because her parents called for independence, they were often jailed by the British. It was not an easy life for a young girl. Indira was a serious child who seemed much older than her years. When Indira was sixteen, her mother died.

3   In 1942, Indira married journalist Feroze Gandhi, with whom she had two sons. Soon after they were married, they were sent to prison by the British. Indira Gandhi's first and only jail sentence lasted from September 11, 1942, until May 13, 1943. When India finally became independent in 1947, Gandhi's father, Jawaharlal Nehru, became the first Indian prime minister. He needed his daughter to act as his official hostess. During this time, Gandhi became better known throughout the country. Her interest in politics grew. The Indian people elected her as a member of parliament. When Nehru died of a stroke in 1964, Gandhi decided to continue in politics and was elected prime minister two years later. She was in power from 1966 to 1977, and again from 1980 to 1984, when she was assassinated.

4   People remember Indira Gandhi for both the good things she did and the mistakes she made. She improved agriculture throughout the country by educating farmers in new farming methods. She often spoke of the rights of women to be in business and politics. She encouraged India to become more industrial by bringing in advisers from different countries to modernize the country. However, in other ways, she was an unpopular leader. She fought with Pakistan. She declared a state of emergency and limited the legal rights of Indian citizens for long periods of time.

5   Indira's biggest mistake led to her death. In the north of the country, a group of Sikhs[1] in the Punjab region wanted independence from India. The Punjab was an

[1]Sikhs (pronounced *Seeks*) are members of an Indian religious group.

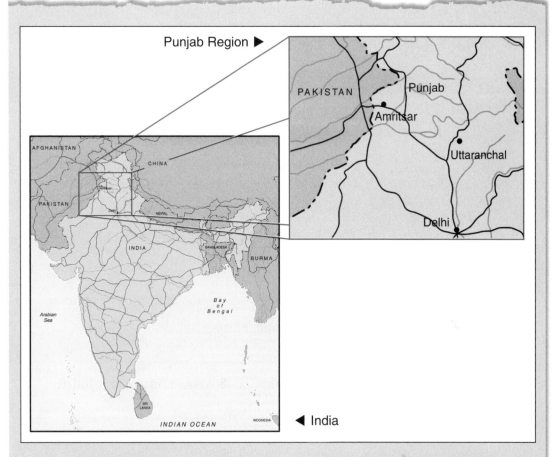

Punjab Region ▶

◀ India

agricultural region with good land and water, and farmers here were well-off compared to many other people in India. However, in the 1980s, a drought began, and the Sikhs in this area became increasingly poor. As life grew more difficult, they listened to the Sikhs who wanted independence. These Sikhs blamed Gandhi's government for the poverty. Then, a group of Sikhs took over the Golden Temple in the Punjab city of Amritsar. The Golden Temple was the religious center for the Sikhs. Sikhs began to fight with non-Sikhs. As the violence increased, the Indian parliament told Gandhi she had to solve this problem.

6   Gandhi had learned the power of peaceful protest from her friend Mohandas Gandhi. Her father, Nehru, also hated violence. However, Indira decided she had to send the army into the temple. She believed it would be a very quick fight and only a few people would be hurt. She was wrong. When the Indian army stormed into the temple, the Sikhs fought back. Hundreds of innocent visitors to the temple were killed, as well as Sikhs. Moreover, the temple itself was badly damaged and religious objects were destroyed. Throughout the country Sikhs and Hindus began to fight. Gandhi's two Sikh bodyguards believed the violence was her fault, and on that morning in October, they killed the woman they were paid to protect. Once again, the world was shocked by the assassination of a national leader.

After You Read

How Well Did You Read?

Work with a partner. Read the statements. Write *T* (true) or *F* (false). Underline the information in the reading that supports your answer.

_____ 1. Indira had an unusual childhood.

_____ 2. Nehru wanted independence for India.

_____ 3. People remember Indira Gandhi only for the good changes she did for India.

_____ 4. The Sikhs wanted to be in control of their region.

_____ 5. The Golden Temple was a political center for the Sikhs.

Check Your Understanding

Answer the questions in complete sentences. Use time phrases.

1. When was Indira Gandhi born?

   _____

2. When did Indira become better known throughout India?

   _____

3. When was Indira Gandhi sent to prison?

   _____

4. When was Indira Gandhi prime minister of India?

   _____

Identifying Supporting Details

Using information from Reading 2, write supporting details for the following main ideas.

1. Indira Gandhi learned about politics as a young child.

   a. Her parents and Mohandas Gandhi talked about India's independence.

   b. _____

   c. _____

2. Gandhi was respected by Indians for the improvements she made as their leader.

   a. _____

   b. _____

   c. _____

3. Indira Gandhi was unpopular for several reasons.

   a. _____

   b. _____

   c. _____

4. The attack on the Golden Temple led to further violence throughout India.

   a. _____

   b. _____

   c. _____

Distinguishing Facts from Opinions

Work with a partner. Read the statements out loud. Discuss which statements are facts and which are opinions. Write *F* (fact) or *O* (opinion).

_____ 1. Indira's family was wealthy.

_____ 2. Mohandas Gandhi often visited Indira's family.

_____ 3. Mohandas Gandhi had a very good influence on Indira's family.

_____ 4. Mohandas Gandhi encouraged the Nehrus to work for independence.

_____ 5. Independence is a good thing to fight for.

_____ 6. Indira Gandhi was a strong leader.

_____ 7. The war with Pakistan was unnecessary.

_____ 8. Indira did not learn very much from Mohandas Gandhi.

_____ 9. Indira believed that the battle against the Sikhs in the Golden Temple would be over quickly.

_____ 10. Indira Gandhi was a good leader who governed during a difficult time.

Recognizing Time Clauses

On page 88, you learned that time phrases such as *during this period, in 1999,* and *three years later* show when things happened. **Time clauses** also show when events happened. A **clause** is a group of words that includes a subject and a verb. Look at the following sentence.

> **When Indira was a very young child,** Mohandas Gandhi visited her home.
> (time clause)

The time clause is introduced by the word *when.* Other words that introduce time clauses include:

- while
- after
- before
- as soon as
- until
- as

A. Combine the pairs of sentences. Use a time word from the list on page 94. If you are not sure about which event happened first, scan the reading to find out. Make other changes if needed.

1. Indira was walking through her garden. Indira was thinking about her plans for the day.
    <u>As Indira was walking through her garden, she was thinking about her plans for the day.</u>

2. Indira's father was the prime minister. Indira's father wanted his daughter to act as his official hostess.
    _____
    _____

3. Indira's father died from a stroke. Indira was interested in politics.
    _____
    _____

4. India became an independent country. The Nehru family met Mohandas Gandhi.

_____

_____

5. Indira ordered the Indian army to take over the Golden Temple. The Indian army moved quickly, and the fighting began.

_____

_____

B. **Read the sentences about the life of Margaret Thatcher, the first woman prime minister of Great Britain. Number the sentences in the correct chronological (time) order. The first one has been done for you.**

_____ 1. Thatcher worked as a research chemist after she graduated from Oxford University.

_____ 2. After she resigned as prime minister, she became a member of the House of Lords.

_____ 3. While she was prime minister, unemployment and poverty increased in the country.

_____ 4. People began to call her "The Iron Lady" when she became prime minister in 1979.

_____ 5. When she resigned in 1990, she had served three terms.

___1___ 6. While Thatcher was a student at Oxford University, she was elected to her first political position—president of the Oxford University Conservative Association.

_____ 7. Before Thatcher was prime minister, she was Secretary of State for Education and Science.

_____ 8. She thought carefully about the future of her political party before she resigned in 1990.

C. Work with a partner. Read out loud the notes about Deng Xiaoping, another important leader in the late 20th century. As you read, try to put the notes into complete sentences.

Example:

Deng Xiaoping was born on August 22, 1904. When he was a young boy, . . .

- Born August 22, 1904
- Young boy—studied in France and Soviet Union
- Young man—interested in politics
- 1949—communist government came to power; Mao Zedong leader; Deng deputy leader
- 1976—Mao died; Deng became leader
- 1977—Deng led the country for next twenty years
- 1980s—Deng did good things for China: encouraged economic growth
- 1989—Deng did bad things: stopped student protestors in Tiananmen Square; many students died
- 1980s—Deng had health problems
- Feb. 19, 1997—Deng died

D. Use the notes to write five sentences about the life of Deng Xiaoping. Be sure to include the following time words: *after, before, while,* and *when.*

1. _____.

2. _____.

3. _____.

4. _____.

5. _____.

Nelson Mandela

Before You Read

Previewing

Nelson Mandela was the first black president of South Africa. He is probably one of the best-known African leaders throughout the world.

Discuss the questions.

1. South Africa has changed a lot in the past few years. What do you know about South Africa in the past? What do you know about South Africa today?

2. Do you think Nelson Mandela has led a happy life? Why or why not?

Now Read

Nelson Mandela

1   On February 11, 1990, Nelson Mandela walked out of prison. He was a free man for the first time in twenty-seven years. Journalists crowded around him, eager to hear him speak. Thousands of people cheered, and Mandela looked a little confused. Then, with his wife by his side, he stood tall and raised his right fist in the traditional freedom salute. The people shouted out in happiness. Their leader was finally free! However, Mandela knew that his journey was not over. The nonwhite people of South Africa were still not free. For the next three years, Mandela worked hard with the political leaders of all the people in South Africa. Together with the president, F.W. de Klerk, Nelson Mandela drafted the first democratic constitution of South Africa. He won the Nobel Peace Prize for his work in 1993. The following year, Mandela was elected as the first black president of South Africa.

2   Mandela's childhood began happily, but life quickly became difficult for him and his family. He was born Rolihlahla Mandela on July 18, 1918, in a small village in the Transkei. This is a beautiful area of South Africa with green hills and sparkling rivers. Mandela's father was chief of the village and was well respected for his wisdom and his love of story telling. Villagers and kings alike asked him for

continued

advice. However, Mandela's father was not free to rule independently. At this time, South Africa was ruled by white South Africans; black South Africans had very little power. When Nelson Mandela was just a small boy, his father refused to obey one of the white magistrates, or local political leaders. The magistrate told Mandela's father he could no longer be chief. The Mandela family had to move from their village, leaving behind their home and their wealth.

3   Like many of the adults in the village, Mandela's father was illiterate because he had never been to school. However, he believed strongly in education and sent his son to school at the age of seven. On Mandela's first day in class, his teacher gave him the English first name of Nelson. For the next few years, Mandela studied hard and became an excellent student. He met other Africans and began to understand more about the world he lived in. It was a difficult world. There was no equality between blacks and whites. It was also a time when traditions were changing. Mandela rebelled against some of these traditions. After his father died, a local chief called Chief Jongintaba looked after Mandela. One day, the chief told Mandela that he had chosen a bride for him. However, Mandela wanted to choose his own wife. In 1941, he ran away to Johannesburg.

4   Living in a large city was very different from living in the countryside. Johannesburg was a growing, dynamic town. People from all over the world lived there. There was great poverty and great wealth. Black people were more independent in the city than in the country. Mandela met people who talked of equality. He met black lawyers who worked hard for the rights of the black South Africans. He decided he wanted to become a lawyer. He wanted to improve the lives of black South Africans.

5   And so the most difficult part of his journey began. As Mandela struggled to get his law degree, the government passed many laws which further restricted the rights of black South Africans. Blacks were only allowed to live in certain "black" areas. They had to carry a pass book. The area where they could live was written in this pass book. If the police caught them in a different area, they could be sent to prison. In addition, schools for black children were inferior to schools for white children. Mandela and his friends began to go to meetings to discuss freedom and equality. These meetings were illegal, and soon Mandela was arrested. Each time the white government arrested him, he defended himself in court and was released. Like his father, he was a strong leader and his reputation grew. As he continued to speak out against inequality, he became well-known, not only throughout South Africa, but throughout the rest of the world. However, in 1963 the South African government charged Mandela with treason,[1] and sentenced him to life imprisonment on Robben Island, an island of rock off the coast of Cape Town.

[1]**treason** = The crime of trying to help enemies of your country or trying to remove your government by violence.

continued

6   Life for the prisoners of Robben Island was extremely hard. Mandela was often kept in solitary confinement. During this time he was alone in his cell. At other times, when he was allowed to be with other prisoners, he and the other men had to do difficult manual work. They broke large rocks into small pieces using only basic gardening tools. Prison food, of course, was poor. Meanwhile, Mandela's children had to grow up without him. In his book, *Long Walk to Freedom: The Autobiography of Nelson Mandela,* Mandela calls these his "dark years."

7   Finally, in 1990, Mandela was released after twenty-seven years in prison. The white government understood that South Africa had to change. They realized that Nelson Mandela was the leader of the black South Africans, and perhaps the only person who could bring peace to the blacks and whites of South Africa. After ten thousand long, hard days in prison, Mandela walked through the gates a free man. As he faced the cheering crowds that day in February 1990, he knew that his walk to freedom was not over, but just beginning.

After You Read

How Well Did You Read?

Complete the time line of Nelson Mandela's life. Write the events from the list in the correct places.

Events:

- Mandela became the first black president of South Africa.
- He won the Nobel Peace Prize.
- Mandela was released from prison.
- Mandela ran away to Johannesburg.

Timeline of Nelson Mandela's Life

Year	Event
1918	Rolihlahla (Nelson) Mandela is born in the Transkei.
1925	He began school.
1941	1. _____
1963	He was sent to prison on Robben Island.
1990	2. _____
1993	3. _____
1994	4. _____

Check Your Understanding

A. Discuss the questions in small groups.

1. How did Mandela's life change when he ran away to Johannesburg?

2. Why do you think Mandela knew that his journey to freedom was not over after he was released from prison?

3. Are there any political leaders in the world today who are in prison for their beliefs?

4. What new information did you learn about South Africa from this reading?

B. Write answers to the questions using complete sentences. Use your own words.

1. What was Mandela's father's position in the village?

   _____

2. Why did he lose this position?

   _____

3. Why do you think Mandela's father believed education was so important?

   _____

4. Why did Mandela run away to Johannesburg?

   _____

5. What was life like for black South Africans at this time?

   _____

6. Why do you think Mandela "struggled" to get his law degree?

   _____

7. Why do you think the government arrested him and sentenced him to life imprisonment?

   _____

8. Why do you think Mandela called his prison time the "dark years"?

   _____

9. Why was he released in 1990?

   _____

10. Why did Mandela win the Nobel Peace Prize in 1993?

   _____

Paraphrasing

Paraphrasing is putting a writer's ideas in your own words, usually in a shorter way. When you paraphrase, you do not copy the author's words. Paraphrasing is a good way to review what you have read.

Examples:

Original sentence: *Mandela rebelled against some of these traditions.*

Paraphrase: Mandela fought against old customs.

Original sentence: *Mandela was often kept in solitary confinement.*

Paraphrase: Mandela was not allowed to be with other prisoners.

Work with a partner. Read the sentences carefully. Then circle the letter of the sentence that is closest in meaning. If you are not sure, quickly scan the reading on pages 97 to 99. Locate the sentence, and reread the surrounding sentences.

1. Journalists crowded around him, eager to hear him speak.

   a. Reporters asked him questions.
   b. Reporters waited quietly for him to speak.
   c. Reporters pushed to get closer to listen to him speak.
   d. Reporters were not interested in this news.

2. Together with the president, F.W. de Klerk, Nelson Mandela drafted the first democratic constitution of South Africa.

   a. Mandela helped write the first laws of the country based on equality for all.
   b. Mandela designed the government buildings in South Africa.
   c. Mandela wrote laws about how to vote in South Africa.
   d. Mandela helped the South African government.

3. Like many of the adults in the village, Mandela's father was illiterate because he had never been to school.

   a. Like other adults in the village, Mandela's father was not a good student.
   b. Like other adults in the village, Mandela's father did not go to school.
   c. Because he rarely went to school, Mandela's father was not intelligent.
   d. Since he and other villagers never attended school, Mandela's father could not read or write.

4. Schools for black children were inferior to schools for white children.

   a. Black children had better schools than white children.
   b. All the schools were the same.
   c. Schools for white children were worse than schools for black children.
   d. Schools for black children were not as good as schools for white children.

5. The South African government . . . sentenced him to life imprisonment on Robben Island. . . .

    a. Mandela had to go to prison for twenty years.
    b. Mandela was sent to prison.
    c. The government told Mandela he had to spend the rest of his life in prison.
    d. The judge told Mandela he would be in prison for a while.

6. When he was allowed to be with other prisoners, he and the other men had to do difficult manual work.

    a. Mandela and the other prisoners worked alone.
    b. All prisoners had to work in the garden.
    c. All the prisoners worked hard doing difficult jobs by hand.
    d. The prisoners were tired because the work was hard.

7. Finally, in 1990, Mandela was released. . . .

    a. After a long time, the government said they were sorry.
    b. After many years, Mandela escaped from prison.
    c. Mandela left prison after a short time.
    d. The government freed Mandela after a long time.

Reading Skill

Highlighting

As you read, it is useful to **highlight** main ideas and major supporting details. This will help you remember the most important information in the reading. You should highlight

- the main ideas.
- the major supporting details.
- important terms or technical vocabulary.

Some students find it helpful to highlight the main ideas with one color and the supporting details with a different color. It is also useful to highlight important vocabulary and write the definitions in the margin.

---

1. Go back to the reading on pages 97 to 99. Read about Mandela's early years. Highlight the main ideas and most important details. Make notes in the margin on any important vocabulary. Then compare your work with a partner's. Have you highlighted the same information?

2. Read about Mandela's adult years before he went to jail. Follow the same steps as in question 1.

3. Read about Mandela's life in jail and after he was released. Follow the same steps as in question 1.

Expanding the Topic

Connecting Reading with Writing

A. Choose one of the following writing exercises. Use vocabulary that you've learned in this chapter to make your writing clear and interesting.

1. Imagine you are Nelson Mandela and you have been in prison for twenty years. Write a letter to your friend explaining how you feel. Tell your friend what it's like being in jail. Describe all the things you miss. Use your imagination as well as the information you have learned about Mandela.

2. Use the notes on page 96 to write a paragraph about the life of Deng Xiaoping. Use both time phrases and time clauses to make your writing clear and interesting. Begin your paragraph like this:

   > Deng Xiaoping was an important Chinese leader. He was born on August 22, 1904. When he was a young boy, . . .

3. Another well-known leader was Cesar Chavez. He worked hard to bring better conditions to agricultural workers throughout the United States. Using these notes, write two paragraphs about the life of this great leader. Use time phrases and time clauses.

   > March 31, 1927, Cesar Chavez born in Arizona; worked on father's small farm as a child.
   >
   > 1929—stock market collapsed; Great Depression began in U.S.
   >
   > Chavez 10 years old—Family lost farm
   >
   > 1937–1944—moved to California—migrant worker; difficult years.
   >
   > 1944—Chavez refused to sit in "Mexican section" of theater. Is jailed for one hour.
   >
   > 1944—Chavez joined U.S. Navy
   >
   > 1948—married Helen Fabela
   >
   > 1950s—Chavez worked for organization to end discrimination against Hispanics
   >
   > 1962—Chavez left his job and started Farm Workers Association to help Hispanic agricultural workers
   >
   > 1960s–1980s—worked to improve living and working conditions of farm laborers; organized boycotts against U.S. grapes. Peaceful protests; successful in getting improvements for farm workers
   >
   > April 23, 1993—died in his sleep
   >
   > April 29, 1993—Chavez's funeral; around 40,000 people attended
   >
   > 1994—President Clinton awarded the Presidential Medal of Freedom to Chavez; Helen and her children accepted the medal.

Exploring Online

Complete the activities using the Internet. If you need help with the computer, or have questions about doing an Internet search, ask your teacher or a classmate to help you.

1. Go online and search for a famous person (world leader, politician, sports star, musician). If you have a library card from a public library, you can go to the library Web site and use their online encyclopedias. Print out the article. Highlight the main ideas and supporting details. Write a paragraph about the person you have chosen. Be sure to use your own words and to write the Web address at the end of the page.

2. Using one of the major Internet search engines, type in "today in history." Using quotation marks around your key words helps you search more accurately. Find out what was happening on this date in the past. Make notes. Using these notes, give an oral presentation to the rest of your class. Remember to tell the class where you got your information.

3. As an alternative to activity 2, find out what was happening the day you were born. Write a paragraph about this special day in history.

4. Nelson Mandela won the Nobel Peace Prize. Go online, and find out more about the Nobel Peace Prize. For example, why is it called the Nobel Peace Prize? When did it begin? Who else has won this prize? Who was the most recent winner?

5. Robben Island is not the only island that has been used as a prison. Choose one of the following island prisons. Search for information about the prison online. Then write a paragraph about it.

   - Alcatraz
   - Andaman Islands
   - St. Helena

The Science of Weather

The three readings in Chapter 5 are about weather-related topics. Reading 1
is a weather forecast for the United States. In Reading 2, you'll learn about
the science of meteorology and how this science has developed over the years.
Reading 3 is an article about hurricanes.

In this chapter, you will practice:

Reading Skills

➡ Previewing a reading
➡ Identifying the main idea
➡ Identifying supporting details
➡ Scanning for details
➡ Highlighting main ideas and supporting details

Vocabulary Skills

➡ Using context clues to understand vocabulary
➡ Choosing the correct dictionary definition

Life Skills

➡ Understanding weather terms
➡ Searching for information on the Internet

Today's Weather

Before You Read

A. Discuss the questions with a partner.

1. In some countries, people talk about the weather a lot. Do you talk about the weather? Is it important for you to know about the weather?

2. Have you ever lived in a place where the weather was different from where you are living now? What was the weather like there?

3. What is your idea of perfect weather?

B. How much weather-related vocabulary do you know? Work with a partner and label each picture. Then, make a list of other weather words you know.

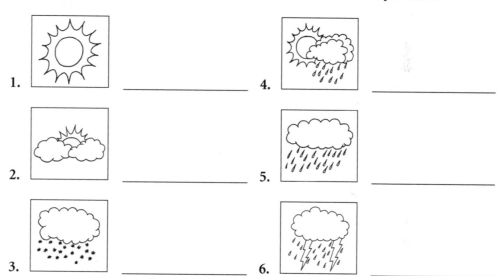

1. _____

2. _____

3. _____

4. _____

5. _____

6. _____

Using Context Clues to Understand Vocabulary

Read the sentence pairs. The words in bold print in the first sentence are in Reading 1 on pages 108 and 109. Underline the word or words in the second sentence that are similar in meaning to those in bold print.

1. There will be **severe** thunderstorms in south Florida for the next twenty-four hours.

   In some areas, the power is already out because of these dangerous storms.

2. It's going to be cold tomorrow in Montana with **a high** of only 32 degrees.

   The highest temperature in neighboring Wyoming will be an even colder 29 degrees.

3. **Light rain** is expected across much of the Northwest.

   Further south, however, these showers could turn into an occasional thunderstorm.

4. Temperatures will **peak at** about 85° this afternoon.

They won't get any higher than that all week.

5. Temperatures **averaged** in the mid-60s all week.

Temperatures were possibly a little higher or lower than 65°, but they were close to 65° all week.

Now Read

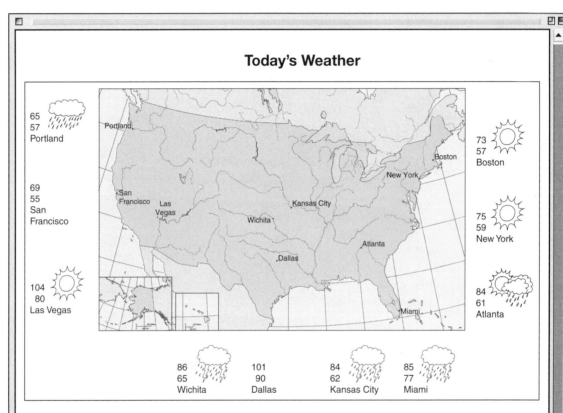

Today's Weather

65 57 Portland

69 55 San Francisco

104 80 Las Vegas

73 57 Boston

75 59 New York

84 61 Atlanta

86 65 Wichita

101 90 Dallas

84 62 Kansas City

85 77 Miami

1   Today's weather in the western United States will generally be good. After a recent unusual hot spell, the Pacific Northwest will be cool with light rain expected, particularly along the coast. Portland will see a high of only 65 degrees! It's a different story in the southwestern states where temperatures will peak at 111 degrees in parts of Texas. Phoenix will see a high of 109 degrees with a possible thunderstorm later this afternoon. This is not going to help the forest fires in Arizona. In the Midwest, temperatures will average in the mid-80s, and there is a severe thunderstorm warning for areas around Kansas City and Wichita. The Gulf States and Miami area will be hot and humid with showers throughout the morning. Temperatures in the Northeast will remain warm with

Washington at 82 degrees and New York a cooler 75 degrees. Fairbanks, Alaska will see a sunny 74 degrees by this afternoon with a low of 55 degrees as a cold front moves in, ending the last two weeks of high temperatures. In Hawaii, temperatures in the islands will range from the 80s to over 100 degrees.

Highs and Lows Across the Nation

Atlanta, GA: Partly cloudy with occasional showers. 84°/61°

Boston, MA: Mostly sunny. 73°/57°

Dallas, TX: Hot and humid. 101°/90°

Las Vegas, NV: Not a cloud in sight. 104°/80°

Miami, FL: Isolated thunderstorms. Showers. 85°/77°

New York, NY: Sunny days ahead. 75°/59°

Portland, OR: Rain, rain, and more rain. 65°/57°

San Francisco, CA: Windy with outbreaks of sun. 69°/55°

Wichita, KS: Severe storms possible. 86°/65°

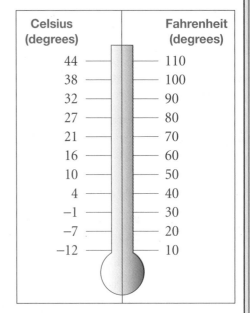

Celsius (degrees)	Fahrenheit (degrees)
44	110
38	100
32	90
27	80
21	70
16	60
10	50
4	40
−1	30
−7	20
−12	10

Long-Term Forecast

2   The National Oceanographic and Atmospheric Administration (NOAA) is predicting that the drought will continue throughout the West until early fall. This is bad news for all those western states battling forest fires. Meanwhile, the National Hurricane Center is getting ready for a busy season this year. Meteorologists are warning East Coast residents to be prepared for several potentially deadly hurricanes to hit the coast before this season is over.

Your Local Forecast

3   For the latest, up-to-date local information, log on to a major weather or news site such as www.weather.com, www.usatoday.com, www.ABCnews.com, www.NBCnews.com, or www.CNN.com.

After You Read

How Well Did You Read?

Read the statements. Write *T* (true), *F* (false), or *N* (not enough information). Underline the information in the reading that supports your answer.

_____ 1. Most of the United States will have calm weather.

_____ 2. The Pacific Northwest is usually cool at this time of year.

_____ 3. Long-term forecasts predict heavy rain in the western part of the United States.

_____ 4. Forest fires are burning in Texas, Miami, and Kansas.

_____ 5. This will be a bad season for hurricanes according to the National Hurricane Center.

Check Your Understanding

Work with a partner. Ask and answer questions about the weather. Use the map on page 108 and information from the reading to help you.

Example:

A: What's the weather like in Dallas, Texas today?

B: It's hot and humid in Dallas today. Temperatures will reach 101 degrees. It's not going to rain.

Scanning for Details

Complete the sentences by quickly scanning the reading on pages 108 and 109 for the answers. Remember to look for key words.

1. Temperatures in Phoenix are going to reach _____ by this afternoon.

2. The state of _____ is fighting forest fires.

3. Kansas City and Wichita will have _____ today.

4. Temperatures in _____ will get up to 74 degrees today.

5. _____ will see a high of 75 degrees and a low of 59 degrees today.

6. The hottest area of the United States today is in the _____.

7. Meteorologists are warning people who live on the _____ that this will be a bad hurricane season.

8. Portland will have a maximum temperature of only _____ today.

Choosing the Correct Dictionary Definition

Sometimes you cannot guess the meaning of a word through context. You need to look it up in a dictionary. Use an English–English dictionary that gives clear definitions and that provides an example of how the word or phrase is used in a sentence. English words often have more than one definition. To choose the correct definition, follow these steps:

1. Get a general idea about the word through context clues in the reading. Decide what part of speech the word is. For example, is it a noun, adjective, or verb?

2. Read the definitions that are the same part of speech you think the word is. Here are the parts of speech and their dictionary abbreviations:
   noun = (*n*)
   verb = (*v*)
   adjective = (*adj*)
   adverb = (*adv*)

3. Choose the definition that is the correct part of speech and that makes sense in the context of the sentence.

A. Read the following sentences from Reading 1. Pay attention to the words in bold print. Then read the dictionary definitions. Follow the steps outlined in the skill box to choose the definition of the word as it is used in Reading 1. Fill in the blank with the definition number.

1. After a recent unusual hot **spell,** the Pacific Northwest will be cool with light rain expected, particularly along the coast.

> **spell**[1] /spel/*v* [I,T] to form a word by writing or saying the letters in the correct order: *My last name is Haines, spelled H-A-I-N-E-S.* | *Our three-year-old is already learning to spell.*
>
> **spell**[2] *n* magic, or the special words or ceremonies used in making it happen: *The witches **cast a spell on** the young prince.*
>
> **spell**[3] *n* a period of a particular type of weather, activity etc.: *We've had a **cold/warm/wet/dry spell** for most of January.*

Definition number: _____

2. Portland will see a **high** of only 65 degrees.

> **high**[1] /haɪ/*adj*
> ►**TALL**◄ having a top that is a long distance from its bottom: *Pike's peak is the highest mountain in Colorado.* | *a high wall.* –opposite LOW[1] –compare TALL
> ►**ABOVE GROUND**◄ being a long way above the ground: *We were looking down from a high window.*
> ►**MORE THAN USUAL**◄ a high amount, number, or level is greater than usual: *clothes selling at **high prices** (=expensive prices)* | *achieving a higher level of productivity*

continued

high² *adv* at or to a level high above the ground: *kites flying* **high in** *the sky*

high³ *n* the highest level, number, temperature, etc. that has been recorded in a particular time period: *The price of gold* ***reached a new high*** *yesterday.* | *a high* (=high temperature) *in the mid 90s*

Definition number: _____

B. Complete the sentences using words or phrases from the list. Use a dictionary to look up words you don't know.

battling	low	range from
drought	meteorologists	severe
high	potentially deadly	warning
hot spell		

1. Scientists who study weather patterns are known as _____.

2. Firefighters were _____ several major forest fires in the western part of the United States yesterday, but fortunately most of the fires are now under control.

3. Rain and cooler temperatures have moved into Alaska, ending its unusual two-week _____ .

4. It's going to be really cold in Chicago tonight with a _____ of −15°F.

5. Lightning from a _____ thunderstorm struck several buildings in Miami yesterday, including an elementary school.

6. This is a _____ to residents in New Haven County: Heavy rain will cause flooding in low areas.

7. People often think desert temperatures are always very hot, but temperatures in these areas _____ very high to extremely cold.

8. Farmers in the Midwest are hoping rain will end the long period of _____ .

9. The National Hurricane Center studies hurricanes to learn more about these _____ weather systems.

10. Parts of Arizona will see a _____ of 104 degrees later this afternoon.

The Science of Meteorology

Before You Read

A. In the past, people had traditional ways of predicting weather. Discuss the following traditional sayings about the weather with a partner. In your opinion, how accurate are these traditional methods of weather forecasting? Share any other sayings you know about the weather.

- Red sky at night, sailor's delight. Red sky in the morning, sailor's warning.
- If the leaves on a tree turn over, bad weather is coming.
- If a Siamese cat turns black in the fall, a cold winter is ahead.
- If the moon has a circle of light around her head, she's going to cry; and her tears will fall as rain in the morning.
- If birds are flying low in the sky, rain is coming.
- When frogs climb up the mango trees, heavy rain is on its way.

B. Reading 2 is a brief history of the science of meteorology—the study of the weather. The reading contains several scientific terms that you need to understand. In a textbook, technical terms will often be boldfaced or explained somewhere on the page. Before you begin to read, look at the boldfaced terms and the definitions provided. This will help you understand the text.

Now Read

The Science of Meteorology

1   In countries like the United States and Britain, people love to talk about the weather. Complete strangers may say to you at the bus stop, "Do you think it's going to rain?" or "What a beautiful day!" In fact, the weather is probably one of the most talked-about topics in the world and for a good reason. Weather affects us in many ways. It affects the food we grow and our health. It affects our travel plans and our

continued

allergies. It affects the clothes we wear and the sports we play. Weather is and always has been an important part of our lives. It is not surprising, therefore, that this subject has fascinated people for thousands of years.

2   People have been trying to understand and influence the weather for a very long time. In ancient times, weather was a matter of life or death. Good weather meant food; droughts or storms resulted in death. People did not understand the natural world, but they tried to influence it. They named gods after the weather, and prayed to them to bring good weather. Egyptians prayed to Ra, the Egyptian god of the sun, while ancient people of Scandinavian countries worshipped Thor, the god of thunder. In the fourth century B.C., two Greek philosophers,[1] Aristotle and Hippocrates, began to analyze weather in a more scientific manner. Aristotle studied different weather patterns, and Hippocrates examined the effects of weather on people's health.

3   The sixteenth century saw the beginning of the scientific revolution, and the science of meteorology began to develop. Galileo invented the first thermometer[2] to measure temperature, and Torricelli invented the barometer[3] to gauge atmospheric pressure.[4] In the eighteenth century, scientific knowledge increased. Scientists identified the major gases in the atmosphere, and Benjamin Franklin discovered atmospheric electricity in his lightning rod experiments. Toward the end of the nineteenth century, the United States Congress told its military bases to keep a record of weather information. When Marconi invented the telegraph[5] in 1895, people could send this data across the country. As Americans continued to move west to settle in new states, they could learn about the coming weather conditions for the first time.

4   The twentieth century saw amazing improvements in meteorology. Radar[6] was first developed for military reasons. However, meteorologists began to use this invention to track severe storms, like hurricanes. If meteorologists could see where the hurricane was heading, they could warn people to leave the area. A second important development was the weather satellite.[7] Hundreds of satellites now circle

[1]**philosopher:** someone who studies about what it means to exist and what good and evil are
[2]**thermometer:** a piece of equipment that measures the temperature of the air, your body, etc.
[3]**barometer:** an instrument for measuring changes in the air pressure and the weather
[4]**atmospheric pressure:** the condition of the air around Earth that affects weather, e.g., high/low pressure
[5]**telegraph:** a method of sending messages by using long and short radio signals to form letters of the alphabet
[6]**radar:** a method of finding the position of things, such as planes, by sending out radio waves; the piece of equipment that does this
[7]**weather satellite:** a communication device that has been sent into space and goes around the Earth, sending and receiving electronic signals

continued

the Earth and show meteorologists how weather is changing, so they can track storms and warn people. Meteorologists now have a global view of the Earth's weather. Finally, computers allow scientists to analyze the huge amount of data collected from radar and satellite technology. When they study the information, they can predict the weather more accurately.

5   The weather continues to affect us all, so people continue to talk about it. There are twenty-four-hour weather channels on TV and radio, and newspapers publish detailed daily forecasts. Go online and you can get weather reports around the world. In fact, the more we learn about meteorology, the more we want to know. So don't be surprised the next time you're waiting for a bus and a stranger asks, "What's the weather going to be like tomorrow?" If you've been online, listened to a radio, watched TV, or read a newspaper, you should know the answer.

After You Read

How Well Did You Read?

Read the statements. Write *T* (true), *F* (false), or *N* (not enough information). Underline the information in the reading that supports your answer.

_____ **1.** The science of meteorology began in the twentieth century.

_____ **2.** Galileo invented the thermometer in the 1600s.

_____ **3.** Scientists developed radar to understand weather patterns more clearly.

_____ **4.** Satellites have improved the weather worldwide.

_____ **5.** Online resources provide the most accurate weather forecasts.

Check Your Understanding

A. Discuss the questions in small groups.

1. What were some of the discoveries between the sixteenth and eighteenth centuries that led to further understanding of the weather?

2. How does the weather continue to affect us? Does it affect us as much as it affected people in the past?

B. Answer the questions in complete sentences. If you are not sure about the answer, go back and reread the article. Use your own words when possible.

1. What's the main idea of this reading?

   _____

2. According to the writer, why do people in some countries talk about the weather so much?

   _____

3. Why did people in the past name gods Ra and Thor?

   _____

4. What's the main idea of paragraph 3?

   _____

5. Why do you think the inventions of Galileo and Torricelli were so important?

   _____

6. Why do you think Congress asked military bases to record the weather?

   _____

7. Why was Marconi's invention important?

   _____

8. Why does the writer think we should know the answer to the question asked in the final paragraph?

   _____

Using Context Clues to Understand Vocabulary

A. Scan the reading on pages 113 to 115 to locate these words. Then read the sentences around the word to find a word or words that are similar in meaning. Write a meaning for the word.

Word (paragraph)	Meaning:
1. analyze (2)	study; examine
2. gauge (3)	_____
3. identified (3)	_____
4. data (3)	_____
5. global (4)	_____
6. forecasts (5)	_____

B. Now write your own sentences using the words from Part A. Think of your own ideas, and don't look back at the reading.

1. Last night I analyzed a short story for my English class.

2. _____

3. _____

4. _____

5. _____

6. _____

Highlighting Main Ideas and Supporting Details

When you read it is important to identify the main ideas and supporting details. Highlighting will help you do this. Look at how the paragraph is highlighted.

Example:

main idea   People have been trying to understand and influence the weather for a very long time. In ancient times, weather was a matter of life or death. Good weather meant food; droughts or storms resulted in death. People did not understand the natural world, but they tried to influence it. They named gods after the weather, and prayed to them to bring good weather. Egyptians prayed to Ra, the Egyptian god

detail #1   of the sun, while ancient people of Scandinavian countries worshipped Thor, the god of thunder. In the fourth century B.C., two Greek philosophers, Aristotle and Hippocrates, began to analyze weather in a more scientific manner. Aristotle studied different

detail #2   weather patterns, and Hippocrates examined the effects of weather on people's health.

A. Highlight the main ideas and supporting details in paragraphs 3 and 4 in Reading 2 on pages 113 to 115. Then compare your work with a partner's. Have you highlighted the same information?

B. Use your highlighted information to complete the following paragraph outlines.

Paragraph 3

main idea: _____

details: 1. <u>Galileo invented the thermometer.</u> _____

           2. _____

           3. _____

           4. _____

           5. _____

Paragraph 4

main idea: _____

details: 1. _____

           2. _____

           3. _____

The Anatomy of a Hurricane

Before You Read

Previewing

A. The long-range forecast from Reading 1 predicts a busy hurricane season. Reading 3 on pages 120 to 123 explains how hurricanes form. Before you read, think about what you know about hurricanes. Discuss the following questions with a partner.

1. Have you ever experienced a hurricane or a violent storm?

2. What happens in a hurricane?

3. What areas of the world are affected by hurricanes?

B. This article is divided by subheadings. Preview the article by reading the title and subheadings. Complete the outline of the reading.

The Anatomy of a Hurricane

1. <u>Cost of a hurricane</u>

2. _____

3. _____

The Anatomy of a Hurricane

1   Today, advances in technology, such as satellites and computers, help meteorologists understand more about global weather patterns than in the past. The weather is no longer a subject of folklore; meteorology is a highly advanced science that results in more accurate forecasts and a greater understanding of weather patterns. For people who live in mild climates, understanding the weather might not be very important unless they are farmers. However, for those who live in areas of the world that are hit by hurricanes, increased understanding of these violent storms can save lives.

What Is the Cost of a Hurricane?

2   Hurricanes are potentially the most dangerous and the costliest of severe weather systems. In 1900, the deadliest hurricane in U.S. history smashed into Galveston, Texas, killing over 8,000 people and causing $30 million in damage. Residents had little warning that this storm was coming. When they realized the storm was a major hurricane, it was too late to evacuate. People were trapped by the storm. Even though residents of the Mississippi Gulf Coast had more warning for Hurricane Camille in 1969, 256 people died and damage was estimated at $1.4 billion. By the time Hurricane Andrew was storming toward the Florida coast in 1992, scientists understood a lot more about weather systems. Their ability to predict these systems had improved significantly. With advance warning, more than one million people along the southern Florida coast were safely evacuated from the area. Although 26 people died in this storm, many more would have died without this warning. Unfortunately, Hurricane Andrew was the most expensive storm in U.S. history with damages costing around $26 billion.

How Does a Hurricane Develop?

3   A hurricane requires two conditions to develop and thrive: large areas of warm water (80°F or above) and wind. These conditions are found in the tropics that lie five degrees to the north and south of the equator. This large area of warm water is the birthplace of violent storms, called typhoons if they occur over the Pacific Ocean, and hurricanes if they happen over the Atlantic Ocean.

continued

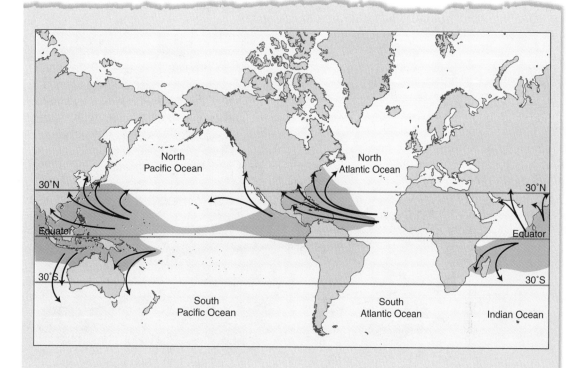

4   There are four stages within the life of a hurricane. First, as the warm, tropical water evaporates,[1] it rises and cools. As it cools, the water vapor condenses[2] into clouds. As the cycle of evaporation and condensation continues, the air begins to move in a circular pattern as it rises to meet the forming clouds. These clouds are clearly visible by satellite and warn scientists that a tropical disturbance is developing.

5   The winds inside the clouds grow stronger when there is a difference in air pressure. As the storm grows, the air at the peak, or top, of the clouds cools rapidly and creates an area of low pressure. The low pressure sucks up the warm air below it, and the wind speed increases. The greater the difference in air pressure, the stronger the wind. The wind inside the storm spins faster and faster, and when these winds reach speeds of between 25 and 38 mph (miles per hour), the storm is called a tropical depression. This is the second stage. The growing storm is now closely monitored by meteorologists who carefully study the data collected by weather satellites.

[1]evaporate: liquid changes to gas

[2]condense: gas turns into liquid

continued

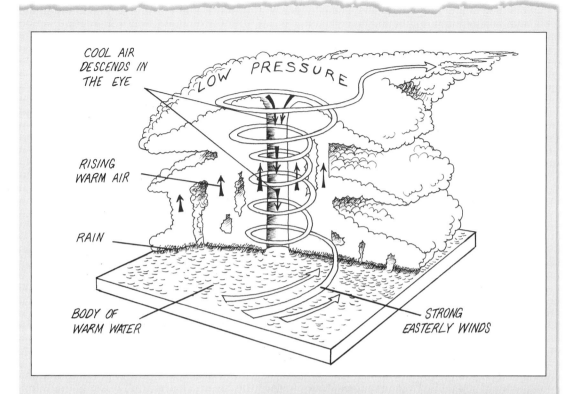

COOL AIR DESCENDS IN THE EYE

LOW PRESSURE

RISING WARM AIR

RAIN

BODY OF WARM WATER

STRONG EASTERLY WINDS

6   As winds increase, they spin around what is known as the eye of the storm. This is the center of the storm system. The eye can be clearly seen on satellites as a black circle within the white swirling cloud mass. The eye itself is very calm. As the winds spin around the eye to speeds above 39 mph, the storm reaches its third stage, known as a tropical storm. At this stage, the World

Meteorological Organization chooses a name for the storm from an alphabetical list. Names alternate between male and female ones. When the winds increase to over 74 mph, the tropical storm enters the fourth stage and becomes a hurricane.

7   In the United States, the hurricane season is from July to October, when ocean waters are warm enough for tropical depressions to begin. Even before this time period, meteorologists at NOAA (the National Oceanographic and Atmospheric Administration) study weather conditions and ocean temperatures to predict how

continued

many hurricanes could occur that season. As July approaches, meteorologists carefully monitor tropical depressions and track these depressions as the wind blows them westward. As a tropical storm or hurricane moves toward land, warnings are broadcast on television and radio, and people begin to prepare for the storm.

What Will Happen in the Future?

8   Scientists continue to learn more about these extreme weather systems. As technology continues to advance, weather forecasts will become more accurate. However, meteorologists are concerned that even with improved forecasts and warning systems, a major hurricane could still lead to a huge loss of life along the Gulf or Atlantic coast. First, they worry because the shorelines of these hurricane-prone areas attract large numbers of people. NOAA estimates 45 million people are living along these coastlines, and new houses continue to be built every day—right on the beaches in many cases. Furthermore, during the peak tourist season, the population of these areas increases dramatically. Evacuation of such a huge number of people is very difficult. The second concern is the technology itself. People can have too much faith in technology. They believe that accurate forecasts and warnings will prevent damage from hurricanes. They also believe this technology will keep them safe. Scientists worry that this attitude could lead to loss of life in a future hurricane. After all, technology allows us to better understand nature, but not to control its power.

After You Read

How Well Did You Read?

Read the statements. Write *T* (true) or *F* (false). Underline the information in the reading that supports your answer.

_____ **1.** Typhoons and hurricanes are the same kind of weather system over different oceans.

_____ **2.** Hurricanes can develop in any area where there is a lot of water.

_____ **3.** In the near future, people will not be hurt by hurricanes because of advanced warning.

_____ **4.** Using scientific data, scientists can estimate how many hurricanes could form in the next season.

_____ **5.** Technology allows scientists to understand and control a storm.

Scanning for Details

A. Complete the two charts. Scan Reading 3 on pages 120 to 123 for the name of each hurricane to find the information.

Deadly Hurricanes of the Past

Name of Hurricane	Date	Number of People Killed	Estimated Damage
(Galveston)	1900		
Camille			
Andrew			

B. Scan the reading for information on the four stages of a hurricane. Look for the key words *first, second, third,* and *fourth*. Then fill in the chart.

The Four Stages of a Hurricane

Stage	Wind Speed	Technical Name
Stage 1		
Stage 2		
Stage 3		
Stage 4		

Check Your Understanding

Read each question and circle the letter of the best answer.

1. Why is meteorology important?

   a. It helps us to control the weather.
   b. It can predict hurricanes and other violent weather patterns.
   c. Understanding the weather can eliminate loss of life.

2. Which sentence is the main idea for paragraph 2?

   a. Hurricanes are very dangerous and can cause millions of dollars in damage.
   b. Scientists have improved hurricane warning systems.
   c. The Galveston hurricane was the worst hurricane in U.S. history.

3. Why did so many people die in the Galveston hurricane of 1900?

   a. Only a few people heard about the warning.
   b. There were too many people to evacuate.
   c. The warning came too late.

4. In 1900, 8,000 people lost their lives to a hurricane; in 1992, only 26 people died because of a hurricane. Why has the number of lives lost fallen over the years?

   a. Fewer people live in hurricane zones today than in 1900.
   b. The hurricanes were not as strong in the 1990s.
   c. Scientists were able to give more advance warnings by 1992.

5. Why do hurricanes develop over the tropics?

   a. The tropics are five degrees north and south of the equator.
   b. The tropics provide the necessary conditions.
   c. The tropics are the birthplace to hurricanes and typhoons.

6. How does an area of low pressure within a storm affect wind speed?

   a. It does not affect the wind speed.
   b. It increases the wind speed.
   c. It decreases the wind speed.

7. Which statement is not correct?

   a. When the eye passes over land, there is little or no wind.
   b. The eye of the storm is the center of the hurricane.
   c. When the eye passes over land, the storm is over.
   d. Winds can spin 75 mph around the eye.

8. What is the difference between a tropical disturbance and a tropical depression?

   a. A tropical depression is a more severe weather condition than a tropical disturbance.
   b. The winds are stronger in a tropical disturbance than in a tropical depression.
   c. There is a greater difference in air pressure in a tropical disturbance than in a tropical depression.

9. What do typhoons and hurricanes have in common?

   a. Both begin over the Pacific Ocean.
   b. Both begin over warm water and move over the Atlantic Ocean.
   c. Both begin over water five degrees to the north and south of the equator.

10. Scientists worry that a hurricane could lead to a huge loss of life in the future. What are the two details that support this main idea?

   a. Many people live and vacation in hurricane areas, and people think technology will keep them safe.
   b. People don't like to leave the beach, especially during the holiday season.
   c. Residents believe that meteorologists' warnings are not accurate, and it's difficult to evacuate large numbers of people.

Using Context Clues to Understand Vocabulary

A. The words in bold print are in Reading 3. The numbers in parentheses refer to the paragraph that contains the word. Use context clues and write the meaning of the words. When you've finished, compare your answers with a partner's.

1. For people who live in **mild climates,** understanding the weather might not be very important unless they are farmers. (1)

   mild climate: _____

2. Hurricanes are **potentially** the most dangerous and the costliest of severe weather systems. (2)

   potentially: _____

3. In 1900, the **deadliest** hurricane in U.S. history smashed into Galveston, Texas, killing over 8,000 people and causing $30 million in damage. (2)

   deadliest: _____

4. By the time Hurricane Andrew was storming toward the Florida coast in 1992, scientists understood a lot more about weather systems. Their ability to predict these systems had improved **significantly.** (2)

   significantly: _____

5. These clouds are clearly **visible** by satellite and warn scientists that a tropical disturbance is developing. (4)

   visible: _____

6. As the storm grows, the air at the **peak,** or top, of the clouds cools rapidly and creates an area of low pressure. (5)

   peak: _____

7. The growing storm is now closely **monitored** by meteorologists who carefully study the data collected by weather satellites. (5)

   monitored: _____

8. The growing storm is now closely monitored by meteorologists who carefully study the **data** collected by weather satellites. (5)

   data: _____

9. However, meteorologists **are concerned** that even with improved forecasts and warning systems, a major hurricane could still lead to a huge loss of life along the Gulf or Atlantic coast. (8)

are concerned: _____

10. After all, technology allows us to better understand nature, but not to control its **power**. (8)

power: _____

B. Complete the following sentences with words from the box.

clearly visible	deadliest	peak	power
concerned	mild climates	potentially	significantly
data	monitored		

1. The _____ of Mount Fuji was _____.
   There wasn't a cloud in the sky.

2. Because of the Internet, the amount of _____ coming into the home has increased _____.

3. Scientists are _____ that if global temperatures increase, areas with _____ will experience drought.

4. HIV (human immunodeficiency virus) is _____ the _____ virus this planet has ever seen.

5. As Mount St. Helens erupted, geologists _____ the _____ of the eruption and the accompanying earthquakes.

C. Work with a partner. What do the following groups of words have in common? The first one has been done for you.

1. tropical storm / tropical depression / hurricane / tropical disturbance

   Answer: <u>They are all stages of a hurricane.</u>

2. broadcast / telegraph / e-mail / telephone

   Answer: _____

continued

3. satellites / radar / barometer / thermometer

Answer: _____

4. Andrew / Camille / Hugo

Answer: _____

5. Aristotle / Galileo / Torricelli / Hippocrates

Answer: _____

D. Read each sentence and the three words or phrases that follow. Two of the answers have a similar meaning to the underlined word or words. Cross out the word or phrase with a different meaning.

1. It's going to be cold tomorrow in Chicago, with a <u>high</u> of only 15 degrees.

~~**a.** hot temperature~~   **b.** peak temperature   **c.** maximum temperature

2. Scientists have been concerned about <u>global</u> warming since the 1980s.

a. international   **b.** worldwide   **c.** national

3. Meteorologists have been <u>tracking</u> the tropical storm on satellite for two days.

a. monitoring   **b.** thinking about   **c.** watching

4. The forecast in the Southeast warned of <u>severe weather</u>.

a. a hurricane   **b.** showers   **c.** a tropical storm

5. The emergency preparedness plan tells residents what they should do in case of a <u>natural disaster</u>.

a. oil spill   **b.** flood   **c.** earthquake

Highlighting and Taking Notes

Imagine you are taking a course in meteorology. Your instructor has asked you to read "The Anatomy of a Hurricane" and then explain how a hurricane develops. Follow these steps to take notes. Use the notes to explain hurricanes.

1. Find the section of the reading that explains how a hurricane develops. Highlight the main ideas and supporting details. Then compare your work with a partner's.

2. Using your highlighted information, write notes on a piece of paper. Use your own words as much as possible. Then compare your notes with a partner's.

3. Make any necessary changes or corrections. Then write your notes clearly on a 3×5 note card. You do not need to write in complete sentences.

4. Work in small groups. Using only your note cards, take turns explaining how a hurricane develops.

Expanding the Topic

Connecting Reading with Writing

Choose either Exercise 1 *or* Exercise 2. Use vocabulary that you've learned in this chapter to make your writing clear and interesting.

1. Find out the weather forecast in your area. You can do this in several ways:

   - Go online to any major news Web site that has information about the weather.
   - Watch your local news on TV.
   - Read the weather section in your local newspaper.

   Now complete the following chart with accurate information about your local weather.

   ### A: Today's Local Weather

Forecast area:
High temperatures:
Low temperatures:
General description:

   Choose a country in a different part of the world. Go online, and find today's weather for that country. Fill in the information. Use the conversion scale on page 109 to convert temperatures to Fahrenheit if necessary.

   ### B: Name of Country: _____

Forecast area:
High temperatures:
Low temperatures:
General description:

   Now write a paragraph contrasting the weather of the countries in charts A and B.

continued

2. Write a paragraph about how either tornadoes or tidal waves are formed. Follow these steps:

- Either do an Internet search to find one or two short articles about your topic, or go to a library and use an encyclopedia such as *The World Book* to find information.
- Download and print the online articles, or make a photocopy of the text articles.
- Preview the articles. Find the section that describes how the weather system forms.
- Highlight main ideas and supporting details.
- Take notes from the highlighted information. Write down the Web address or the name, title, and publisher of the book.
- Using only your note cards, write your paragraph. Include the Web address or the title, author, and publisher of the book at the bottom of the page.

Exploring Online

Complete the activities using the Internet. If you need help with the computer, or have questions about doing an Internet search, ask your teacher or a classmate to help you.

1. Scientists are concerned that the Earth's temperature is increasing. This is known as global warming. Go online and use a major search engine to search "global warming." Find an article that clearly explains this. Using the note-taking techniques you have practiced in this chapter, answer the following questions:

   a. What is global warming?
   b. What are the causes of global warming?

   Remember to include the Web address at the end of your writing.

2. Do a search for earthquakes or volcanoes. Find out what causes an earthquake or a volcanic eruption. Take notes or print out the Web page and highlight information. Make an outline for your writing. Be sure to include a specific example of an earthquake or volcanic eruption to make it clearer and more interesting for your reader. Include the Web address.

3. You are a meteorologist working for a twenty-four-hour radio weather station. Your job is to provide the "Weather Around the World" report each day at noon. Go online and find information about the world's weather today. Using note cards, prepare a two-minute oral presentation. You may use your note cards during your report. Reading 1 of this chapter may give you ideas about how to begin.

Employment Issues

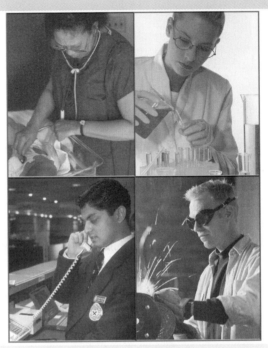

The readings in Chapter 6 are about employment-related subjects. Reading 1 explores two online resources. The second reading is part of the classified section in a newspaper. Reading 3 includes a dialogue and two résumés.

In this chapter, you will practice:

Reading Skills

➡ Previewing a reading

➡ Interpreting charts and numbers

➡ Scanning for details

Vocabulary Skills

➡ Choosing the correct word form

➡ Using context clues to understand vocabulary

Life Skills

➡ Understanding help wanted abbreviations

➡ Describing personal skills

➡ Résumé writing

➡ Researching interview questions online

Looking to the Future: Online Resources for Tomorrow's Jobs

Before You Read

A. Discuss the questions with a partner.

1. Look at the photos on page 131. What jobs do these people have? (Check the bottom of this page for the answers.)

2. What job does (or did) your mother or father have? How many years has he or she worked at this job? Has he or she had different jobs?

3. What job do you want in the future? Do you think you will have the same career all your life?

4. How do people find jobs today where you are living now?

5. If you are working right now, how did you find out about your job?

B. Look at the careers listed in the following chart. Do you think there will be many jobs in these careers in the future? If you think there will be many jobs, check (✓) **good** in the Future Outlook column. If you think there will be some jobs, check **OK**. If you think there will not be many jobs in this career, check **poor**. Then write a reason to explain each answer. Finally, add two more careers to the chart and mark your predictions about them under Future Outlook.

Career	Future Outlook			Reason
	good	OK	poor	
Nurse				
Teacher				
Computer specialist				
Bookkeeper				
Car mechanic				
Dentist				
Others:				
_____				
_____				

p. 131: (top row) nurse, lab technician; (bottom row) receptionist, welder

Previewing Vocabulary

These words are in Reading 1. Read the words and their definitions. Then choose the best word to complete each sentence.

changed dramatically	changed a lot in a short time
earnings	the money you get by working
guidance	helpful advice about work, education, etc.
occupations	jobs
opportunities	occasions when it is possible for you to do something; chances to get a job
outlook	what is expected to happen in the future
resources	things you use to make a job or activity easier
welder	a person who joins together metal by heating the edges and pressing them together when they are hot

1. Because people are living longer, the _____ for health care workers is excellent.

2. Many people need career _____ before they choose a new occupation.

3. My life _____ after I got a job. I was able to buy a car, move into my own apartment, and make a lot of friends at work.

4. A community college usually has an employment center with many _____ to help you choose a career.

5. Is college worth it? Yes! College graduates have higher _____ than high school graduates.

6. The _____ wore thick gloves so the hot metal wouldn't burn his hands.

7. People with computer technician certificates will find that there are many employment _____.

8. Desktop publishing is one of the fastest-growing _____ at the moment.

Now Read

Looking to the Future: Online Resources for Tomorrow's Jobs

1   Alex, a recent Russian immigrant, reported the following experience: "My father was a welder in Russia, and he taught me to weld. He worked in one factory all his life. It was run by the government. If the factory needed any new workers, the supervisor put up a list on the outside wall. When I finished my training, I went to my father's factory. I looked at the list and saw the factory needed a welder. I took my papers to the office, and the supervisor checked them. He then told me where to go to start work. There was no interview. I had no choice because I was a welder, and there was only one factory near where I lived. Now I'm here in Chicago, and there are so many choices and so much information, I feel very confused. I don't want to be a welder all my life, but I'm not sure what I do want to be. I don't know where to begin."

2   The world of employment has changed dramatically in the last twenty years. Like Alex, many people need guidance in choosing a career. Fortunately, there is a lot of information on the Web about job opportunities, earnings, and how to get a job. You can search on the Web to find out about new opportunities in careers, such as computers, communication, and publishing. Many Web sites also provide information about how to apply for a job. There are sample résumés, letters of application, and interview questions to help people get a job. With all this information available, it's not surprising that people can feel confused. So if you're like Alex, and you're ready to enter a training program, start your first job, or change careers, where do you begin?

3   *The Occupational Outlook Handbook* and *America's CareerInfonet* are good resources. They are published by the U.S. Department of Labor and are regularly updated. *The Occupational Outlook Handbook* is available as a book and online. *America's CareerInfonet* is online only. Not only is information provided about the United States as a whole, but readers can easily search for information about their particular state. You can read about the fastest-growing occupations in the area where you live and find out the average wages in these occupations. If you are already interested in a career, you can find out what it is like to work in that career, the earnings you can expect, and the training you will need.

continued

4   Take, for example, Nadia's situation. Nadia was a doctor's assistant in Iran, and her goal in the United States is to become a nurse. However, she needs to work while she is studying nursing. She is interested in becoming a medical assistant to help work her way through college. She goes online to *The Occupational Outlook Handbook* and searches under "medical assistant." She is happy to read that this is expected to be one of the fastest-growing careers through 2010. Moreover, job opportunities are even better for people with experience. She discovers that medical assistants not only have administrative duties, but clinical responsibilities as well. For example, a medical assistant answers telephones, greets patients, files records, and schedules appointments, as well as draws blood, calls in prescriptions, and prepares patients for x-rays. Nadia decides this job will be interesting and will also provide excellent experience for her nursing career.

5   *The Occupational Outlook Handbook* and *America's CareerInfonet* are just two examples of Web sites that can help you plan a new career. There are many other excellent Web sites available. When you have found information about some different careers and the outlook for those careers, you will be ready to talk to career advisers. Choosing your future career is an extremely important decision. It's worth taking the time and finding out as much information as you can.

After You Read

How Well Did You Read?

Work with a partner. Read the statements. Write *T* (true), *F* (false), or *N* (not enough information). Underline the information in the reading that supports your answer.

_____ 1. Alex's experience of getting a job in the former Soviet Union was very different from how most people get a job in the United States today.

_____ 2. Information is necessary, but too much information can be confusing.

_____ 3. Searching online did not help Nadia make a decision.

_____ 4. *The Occupational Outlook Handbook* is the best resource for career guidance.

_____ 5. It's a good idea to do some research before you choose your career.

Check Your Understanding

Circle the letter of the best answer.

1. Why does the writer begin with the story about Alex in paragraph 1?

   a. To tell the reader this article is about Russian immigrants.
   b. To show that life in Russia today is very different from in the past.
   c. To introduce the idea that choosing a career today can be confusing.

2. What's the main idea of paragraph 2?

   a. Getting a job has become more difficult the past few years.
   b. There is a lot of information online about getting jobs, but it can be confusing.
   c. Web sites can help you get a job, so getting a job is easier than it was in the past.

3. According to paragraph 3, which statement about *The Occupational Outlook Handbook* and *America's CareerInfonet* is *not* correct?

   a. The sites provide information about what most people earn in different occupations.
   b. The sites give information about which careers are growing the quickest.
   c. You must call for a copy of the handbooks.

4. Which sentence is closest in meaning to the following sentence from paragraph 3?

   Not only is information provided about the United States as a whole, but readers can easily search for information about their particular state.

   a. There is only information about America in general.
   b. Readers can find information about the national and state job markets.
   c. Readers can only find information about their own state.

5. Why does the writer include the example about Nadia?

   a. to show that the two Web sites are the best online resources
   b. to show how useful these Web sites can be
   c. to show that Nadia knows how to use these Web sites

6. Which sentence is closest in meaning to the following sentence from paragraph 4?

   She discovers that medical assistants not only have administrative duties, but clinical responsibilities as well.

   a. Medical assistants have more administrative responsibilities than clerical duties.
   b. Medical assistants have more clinical duties than responsibilities.
   c. Medical assistants have both clinical and administrative responsibilities.

Interpreting Charts and Numbers

Writers often use charts and numbers to give information that supports a reading. Interpreting charts and numerical, or number-based, information will help you understand readings better.

To understand charts, first you need to read and understand the title and headings in the chart.

To talk about the information in a chart you need to use verbs that describe changes in numbers, for example:

> The need for nurses *is growing.* The outlook is good.

> The number of bookkeepers *is decreasing* because employers are using computers for this job. The outlook is not good.

Here are some verbs that describe changes in numbers:

grow   rise   increase
decline   fall   decrease

A: Ten Fastest Growing Occupations in the United States

Number	Occupation	Number of Jobs in 2000	Number of Jobs in 2010	% Change	Earnings
1	Computer software engineers	380,000	760,100	100	$$$$
2	Computer support specialists	505,600	995,900	97	$$$
3	Computer systems software engineers	316,900	601,200	90	$$$$
4	Network systems administrator	228,500	415,700	82	$$$$
5	Data analysts	118,700	210,600	77	$$$$
6	Desktop publishers	38,000	63,300	67	$$$
7	Database administrators	106,000	175,900	66	$$$$
8	Personal and home care aides	413,600	672,200	62	$
9	Computer systems analysts	431,400	689,200	60	$$$$
10	Medical assistants	328,600	515,800	57	$$

Key to Earnings (in whole dollars)

$$$$	very high: $39,700 and over	$$	low: $18,500 to $25,759
$$$	high: $25,760 to $39,699	$	very low: under $18,499

continued

B: Occupations in the United States with Declining Employment

Number	Occupation	Number of Jobs in 2000	Number of Jobs in 2010	% Change	Earnings
1	Railroad operators	21,900	8,600	−61	$$$
2	Shoe machine operators	9,100	4,200	−54	$
3	Telephone operators	53,600	34,700	−35	$$$
4	Loan interviewers and clerks	138,900	100,600	−28	$$$
5	Motion picture projectionists	11,100	8,100	−27	$
6	Rail-track layers and maintenance equipment operators	11,800	8,700	−26	$$$
7	Meter readers	48,800	36,100	−26	$$$
8	Farmers and ranchers	1,293,700	965,500	−25	$$$
9	Radio mechanics	6,900	5,300	−24	$$$
10	Shoe and leather workers and repairers	18,900	14,800	−21	$

Key to Earnings (in whole dollars)

$$$$	very high: $39,700 and over	$$	low: $18,500 to $25,759
$$$	high: $25,760 to $39,699	$	very low: under $18,499

A. Read Charts A and B. Then read the statements. Write *T* (true), *F* (false), or *N* (not enough information).

_____ 1. The number of medical assistants is expected to increase by 57%.

_____ 2. Data analysts will earn more than database administrators.

_____ 3. The number of desktop publishers will fall from 63,300 to 38,000.

_____ 4. The number of farmers and ranchers will fall to 965,500.

_____ 5. According to the chart, there will be more jobs for personal and home care aides than for computer systems software engineers.

B. Answer the questions about Charts A and B.

1. Which occupation is expected to have the most jobs available in 2010?

   _____

2. Which occupation is expected to have the highest growth rate (+ percent change)?

   _____

3. Which occupation is expected to have the fewest jobs available in 2010?

   _____

4. Which occupation is expected to have the biggest decline in job openings (– percent change)?

   _____

5. Which four occupations are expected to have the lowest earnings?

   _____

C. Write statements to describe the outlook for the following occupations. Use information from Charts A and B, and use verbs that describe changes in numbers.

1. computer software engineers _The need for computer software engineers is growing. The outlook is good._

2. telephone operators _____

   _____

3. desktop publishers _____

   _____

4. medical assistants _____

   _____

5. radio mechanics _____

   _____

6. farmers and ranchers _____

   _____

continued

7. railroad operators _____

_____

8. personal and home care aides _____

_____

Help Wanted

Before You Read

Life Skill

Understanding Help Wanted Abbreviations

Many people start their search for a job in the help wanted section of the local newspaper. This section lists job openings. Job advertisements use as few words as possible. Some words are omitted, or left out, and others are abbreviated or shortened. You need to understand the abbreviations in order to understand the advertisements.

Example:

Welders: must have exp. Cert. req. Exc. Salary + benefits DOE. FT and PT avail. Call Mike: (001–101–0110)

exp = experience

Cert. req. = certification required

DOE = depends on experience

Work with a partner to see how many abbreviations you know. Share your answers with the class. Make sure you know all the abbreviations before you begin the reading.

admin. asst. _____

FT _____

PT _____

w/e _____

flex hrs _____

exc. _____

salary DOE _____

min. _____

qual. _____

exp. req. _____

$32k _____

prof. _____

BR _____

auto tech. _____

cert. _____

locs. _____

ref. req. _____

exp. pref. _____

Previewing Vocabulary

These words are in Reading 2 on page 143. Read the words and their definitions out loud with a partner. Then choose the best word to complete each sentence.

Word	Definition
applicants	people who apply for a job
benefits	services you get as part of your salary, i.e., medical insurance, paid holidays, retirement pension
dependable	someone you can trust
flexible	can easily change
long-term	continuing for a long time into the future
minimum	the smallest possible amount
preferred	an advantage, but not required
proficient in	good at doing something
required	must have, necessary
résumé	written description of your education and experience

1. Only experienced _____ should apply.

2. To apply for this job, please send your _____ to the address below.

3. Drug testing is _____ for all employees.

4. Students like _____ hours so they can change their work schedule to fit their school schedule.

5. Office administrators must be _____ in Word and Access.

6. Experience with Asian cooking is _____, but not required.

7. _____ are available to spouse and children.

8. It is important to plan for future business by developing _____ goals.

9. The _____ qualifications are a bachelor's degree and three years of experience. You must have these to apply for the job.

10. Tran was promoted to a supervisor because he was so _____.

Now Read

Take turns reading the following employment advertisements out loud with a partner. When you come to an abbreviation, read the full meaning.

For example, in the first ad, "Admin. Asst. Multiskilled person to assist busy prof. office" would be read as:

Administrative Assistant. Multiskilled person to assist busy professional office.

Help Wanted

Admin. Asst.
Multiskilled person to assist busy prof. office. Good people skills a must. General office and admin. duties. Real estate exp. pref. Proficient in Word & Excel. Organized, dependable, detail-oriented. Salary to $27k. Exc. benefits. E-mail résumé to jmcpartners@nom.com

Resident Apartment Manager
Needed for 34-unit complex. Must be experienced in leasing, basic maintenance, and bookkeeping. Good customer relations a must. 2 BR unit + utilities + salary DOE. References. Drug testing required. Call Sandy (415) 774–1000

Auto Technician
Exp. Auto tech wanted. Cert. required. 4 possible locs. Top pay, benefits, 401K.[1] Flex. hrs. E-mail résumé to AutoAce@zero.com

[1]401K = retirement investment plan

Construction
Work available for exp. siders and roofers. Immediate + long-term employment opportunities. Multifamily construction projects in SW area. Must be able to travel. Exc. salary + benefits + travel allowance. Call Mike (417) 333–4414. Drug Free Workplace.

Engineer: Section Manager
Global consulting engineering company seeks qualified Materials Testing engineer. Based in NY. Extensive travel required. Min. quals: BA or MA in Civil Engineering + min. 7 years exp. with min. 4 years managerial exp. Must have excellent communication + financial skills. Responsibilities include: developing marketing and business goals, maintaining budget, developing and maintaining client base, lead supervision of team from 6–8 engineers + staff. Exc. salary + benefits. Qualified applicants only

send résumé to Testingcorp@aba.com Testing Corporation is an Equal Opportunity Employer.

Restaurant
Southwest College of Arts is accepting résumés for PT cook to work w/e in international dormitory. Applicants should have exp. in Asian cooking + enjoy trying new recipes. No formal qual. req. Must have exp. in cooking for up to 30. Salary DOE. Call Mariko (777) 455–7836. Ref. req.

Teacher—Preschool
New 24-hr. preschool + child-care facility seeks Certified Early Childhood Ed. Teacher. Must have min. 3 years exp. Enthusiastic, creative, and independent worker. Spanish or Korean an advantage. Salary / benefits DOE. Also need night shift personnel: $10–15/hr. Drug Testing + police check req. Call Maria (910) 478–4444.

After You Read

How Well Did You Read?

Read the statements. Write *T* (true), *F* (false), or *N* (not enough information). Underline the information in the reading that supports your answer.

_____ 1. Most of these jobs require some experience.

_____ 2. You should telephone for applications for all the positions.

_____ 3. Some of the jobs involve travel.

_____ 4. A second language is an advantage for the preschool teacher.

_____ 5. The cook will earn less than the preschool teacher.

Check Your Understanding

Work in small groups. Discuss the questions and share your answers with the class.

1. What skills does an administrative assistant need, according to the advertisement?

2. The advertisement for a resident apartment manager says that basic maintenance and good customer relations are required. What does this mean?

3. Which advertisements say they require drug testing? Why do you think some advertisements say this while others do not?

4. Why do you think a lot of travel is required for the engineer's position? Would you like a job that required travel? Why or why not?

5. The advertisement for a teacher says the preschool/child-care facility is open twenty-four hours. Why would a child-care center need to be open at night?

Scanning for Details

Read the questions. Then scan the reading to find the answers. Complete this exercise as quickly as possible.

1. How many years of experience in management are required for the engineering job?

   _____

2. Which positions state that references are required?

   _____

3. Which positions offer benefits?

   _____

4. Which days will the cook work for Southwest College of Arts? _____

The positions of

5. Two positions require travel. Which are they? _____

6. Which company says it is an Equal Opportunity Employer? *Texting Corporation*

7. Which position offers flexible hours? _____

8. What shifts are available at the preschool? *Resident Apartment*

9. Which job offers an apartment as part of the salary package? *manager offers an apartment as part of the salary pac*

10. Which position requires a degree? _____

Life Skill

Describing Personal Skills

When you apply for a job, you have to talk about your skills. You need to be able to clearly communicate what you are good at doing. There are several ways to do this:

I have good communication skills.

I can fix things.

I'm good at working with children.

I am experienced in working with people from diverse backgrounds.

I enjoy working independently.

well
very organiser

positive

A. Work in small groups. Practice answering these questions. Use examples from the skill box to help you.

I have excellent attitude,
I have skills
solve problem

1. What are you good at doing?

2. What skills do you have?

3. What are you interested in doing?

4. What do you enjoy doing?

5. What can you do?

outgoing
paitient

I like work with com. read a lot, I like spo
sympathetic
I am veray pleasant person   I have excel
freindly   I like lary new thigs attitude
I am going to   tem worker
become   a nurse

B. Complete the sentences using information from Reading 2 on page 143. Use the examples from the skill box to help you.

1. A person applying for the administrative position should enjoy

_____.

2. A person applying for the apartment manager job must be experienced in

_____.

3. An auto technician must have _____.

4. The engineer must enjoy _____.

5. The cook must be good at _____.

Vocabulary Skill

Choosing the Correct Word Form

Many words have different forms. Some verbs, for example, can be changed to nouns, adjectives, or adverbs. The following sentences show three different word forms of the word *abbreviate*.

> Newspaper advertisements often use **abbreviations**. (noun)

> Writers usually **abbreviate** "Mister" to *Mr.* (verb)

> My boss asked me to rewrite the report in an **abbreviated** form. (adjective)

Understanding and learning different word forms is a good way to increase your vocabulary.

Choosing the Correct Word Form

A. Complete the following sentences by choosing the correct word form. The number in the chart corresponds to the sentence number below.

	Verb	Noun	Adjective
1.	apply	application	applied *are person* *for things*
2.	confuse	confusion	confused / confusing
3.	administer	administrator	administrative
4.	employ	employment	employed
5.	expand	expansion	expanding
6.	grow	growth	growing
7.	inform	information	informative
8.	populate	population	populated
9.	require	requirement	required
10.	supervise	supervisor	supervised

1. You can pick up an _____ application _____ at the information desk.

2. Applying for a job in a new city can be very _____ confusing _____.

3. Young discovered that she really enjoyed her _administrative_ duties.

4. Large companies like Cisco Systems _____ huge numbers of people.

5. _Expanding_____ opportunities in medical occupations have resulted in more colleges offering training in these areas.

6. There is _____ growing _____ concern that more people will lose jobs because of the weak economy.

7. Since the development of the Internet, more _____ is easily available to people in their homes.

8. New York City is a heavily _____ populated _____ area.

9. One _____ for this job is several years of experience.

10. The manager had to _____ supervise _____ several staff members, and she found that this was the hardest part of her job.

continued

B. Now use these words in your own sentences. Your sentences should be about employment.

1. apply <u>When you apply for a job, you usually need a résumé.</u>

2. confused _____

3. administrative _____

4. employ _____

5. expand _____

6. grow _____

7. informative _____

8. population _____

9. required _____

10. supervisor _____

| Reading 3 | *Part A: Where Do I Start?* |

Before You Read

Predicting

Reading 3, Part A on pages 149 and 150 is about four students. They are talking about the problems they face in getting a job. Before you read, write down three problems you think the students might experience as they try to get a job.

1. _____

2. _____

3. _____

Where Do I Start?

Four students are studying English as a Second Language at a community college. All four are looking for jobs. Three are resident students and therefore can legally work; the fourth, Mohammed, is an international student. Because he is here on a student visa, he cannot work off campus. However, he is allowed to work on campus for a maximum of twenty hours a week. The four students are having coffee in the student lounge and talking about finding a job.

Claudia: I need some help. I have to get a job soon, but I don't know where to start. I don't have any experience here, and I don't have any skills. I need a job, but who needs me?

Irina: I'm looking for a job as well. In fact, I've just sent off my résumé to a software business near the college. I hope I get an interview soon.

Claudia: How did you write your résumé? I know I need to write one, but it's hard to write it in English. In fact, writing a résumé is hard even in my own language. And remember, I don't have experience or skills. It's going to be a short résumé!

continued

Irina:	Claudia, you have more skills and experience than you think. My career guidance adviser helped me figure that out. First he made me write down a list of the jobs I did in Ukraine. He told me to do this in Ukrainian. Then he told me to think about what I'm good at doing and make a list. I wrote that in my own language as well.
Mohammed:	Can your adviser speak Ukrainian?
Irina:	No! But when I finished, I showed him the three pages of notes, and he said my problem was not a lack of experience. My problem was translating that experience into English. He was right.
Mohammed:	How did you translate it? I've tried translating the work I did with my father into English, but I couldn't. There are too many technical terms I don't know.
Irina:	One of my friends helped me do a general translation. Then I went and talked to my adviser again. She helped me explain some of the more technical skills I have. It's important to use exactly the right words in a résumé.
Claudia:	So you included experience from Ukraine? I thought I had to have experience here. I worked for five years in Brazil. I'm going to try beginning the same way you did, Irina. Then, I also have a friend at the university who can help me.
Vinh:	You're lucky. My English is not very good, and I also have another problem. I came here straight from high school in Vietnam. I've never had a job. I don't have any experience. To make it worse, I don't even know what kind of job I want.
Mohammed:	I helped my father with his business while I was a student in Saudi Arabia, but it wasn't a real job. Now there is a job on campus in the bookstore. It's only part-time, so I can apply for it. But I don't have a résumé. My father is telling me I must get a job to help out with the cost of tuition. I need this job, but the advertisement said experience is required.
Vinh:	Hey, look at the time! We need to get to class. Let's get together later and talk more about how to get a job.

After You Read

Check Your Understanding

Work in small groups.

1. Irina, Claudia, Mohammed, and Vinh are having difficulties finding a job.
   What are the problems? Read the dialogue one more time and underline the
   problems. Then complete the Problem column in the chart below. You don't
   need to write in complete sentences.

Student	Problem	Solution
Irina	her problem was translating experience into English.	friends helped her to do general translation important to use exactly the right words in a resume
Claudia	doesn't know where to start, no experience, no skills, write resume	she has a friend at the university, she worked for five years in Brazil.
Mohammed	International student cannot work off campus, max. 20 hours a week, write resume	he found a job on campus in the bookstore, only p/t.
Vinh	bad English, never had a job, no experience	After class he want to talk more about how to get a job

mature

2. Irina found solutions to her problem. Read the dialogue and highlight her
   solutions. Write them in the Solution column next to her name.

3. Now look at the problems facing Claudia, Mohammed, and Vinh. The reading
   does not give direct solutions to their problems. Work in a group. Think of
   some solutions to these problems. Write these solutions in the chart. Share
   your group's answers with the class.

Before You Read

Résumé Writing

A **résumé** is a written description of an applicant's experience and education. There are several different ways to organize a résumé. People who have a lot of experience usually focus on this experience. They list the companies they have worked for and the duties they have performed. On the other hand, people who do not have very much experience, or perhaps have no experience at all, often use a skills-based résumé. A skills-based résumé focuses on what the applicant is good at doing.

Work in small groups. Discuss these questions.

1. Have you ever written a résumé? Did you organize it by experience or by skills?

2. Do you need a résumé right now? If not, when will you need one? Do you think it will be difficult to write your résumé?

Irina Ivanovich
111 Main St.
Sims Town, IL 00001
(222) 333–3331
iivan@anyadress.com

Goal: Seeking position as administrative assistant in software development company

Education: 2004: Associate's Degree in Business Technology
Sims College, Sims Town, IL

2003: Certification in Word, Excel, PowerPoint

1999: Technical Certificate in Office Administration
Ukraine College, Ukraine

Experience: December 2003–present
Office Assistant, Sims College, Sims Town, IL
Duties: answering phone in busy office, responding to inquires, word processing and editing, creating spreadsheets, tracking budgets

March 2002–November 2003
Work-Study Student, English as a Second Language Program, Sims College
Duties: prepared mailing lists, filed records, answered phone, operated photocopier and international fax

September 1999–August 2000
Office Administrator, Zlat Company, Ukraine
Duties: answered busy phones, handled correspondence, did filing, took dictation, made travel arrangements, tracked budgets

стенографія
short hand
визначати на листи

Skills: Fluent Ukrainian and Russian. Proficient in Polish

References: Available on request

After You Read

How Well Did You Read?

Read the statements. Write *T* (true), *F* (false), or *N* (not enough information).
Underline the information in the reading that supports your answer.

_F_ 1. Irina is unemployed at the moment.

_T_ 2. Irina began her college education in her former country.

_F_ 3. Her first experience in working in the United States was as an office assistant.

_T_ 4. Irina has experience working with numerical information.

_N_ 5. Irina has good references.

Check Your Understanding

Answer the questions in complete sentences. Use correct verb tenses.

1. When did Irina finish her Technical Certificate program in Ukraine?

   Irina had finished her Technical Certificate program in Ukraine in 1999.

2. What do you think she did between 2000 and 2002?

   I think she was studing

3. What was she doing in October 2003?

   She was work-study Student ESL program in Sims College

4. When did she begin working in her current position?

   She began working on her current position in December 2003

5. Why do you think Irina is applying for a new job?

   She will get better selary and benefits.

Before You Read

In Reading 3, Part A, Vinh talks about his problems finding a job. His English is still a little weak, and he has no work experience. Meanwhile, there is a job opportunity at a local home improvement store, and Vinh wants to apply. After talking to a career adviser, Vinh decides to write a skills-based résumé. This style of résumé will focus on what he is good at doing rather than on his lack of work experience.

Make a list of skills that would be helpful in getting a job at a home improvement store.

Plumbing and paiting

1. good knowledge of basic electrical wiring,
2. good at using variety of electrical tools and *spray*
   paiting equipment
3. experienced in remodeling
4. good at working with customers;
5. good listening skills, friendly
   professional manners *trait*
   behavior

depeudeble
imedgine di

Vinh Nguyen
222 South Avenue
Sims Town, IL 00001
(333) 222-2221
vnguy@anyemail.com

Goal: Seeking an entry-level position in home improvement store

Education: 2002–present: Sims College, Sims Town, IL
Courses completed include: English as a Second Language, Introduction to Word and Excel, Intermediate Algebra, Electrical Technician's Certificate
2000: High School Diploma, HCM School, Vietnam

Skills: **Languages**
- Fluent in Vietnamese
- Proficient in English and Thai

Home improvement / mechanical
- Good knowledge of basic electrical wiring, plumbing, and painting (exterior and interior)
- Good at using variety of electrical tools and spray painting equipment
- Experienced in remodeling (remodeled old house for resale)

Retail
- Good at working with customers (helped customers in father's electrical store in Vietnam)
- Experienced in using cash register

People
- Good at working with people from diverse backgrounds
- Excellent listening skills; friendly and professional manner

References: Available on request

After You Read

How Well Did You Read?

Read the statements. Write *T* (true), *F* (false), or *N* (not enough information).
Underline the information in the reading that supports your answer.

_____T_____ **1.** Vinh has no experience that would be useful for the job he wants.

_____F_____ **2.** Vinh is hard to understand because of his English.

_____T_____ **3.** Vinh will get this job because he has good skills.

_____N_____ **4.** Vinh is comfortable working with a variety of tools.

_____T_____ **5.** Vinh believes he is good at working with people from different countries.

Applying What You Have Learned

Work in small groups.

1. Preparing a résumé is one of the first steps to finding a job. Talk about the challenges you face in preparing a résumé and finding a good job. Do you face the same problems talked about in Reading 3, Part A? Write down the problems you face in the chart that follows.

2. Now talk about solutions. Help each other think of ways to overcome some of these problems. Write down the solutions.

3. When you have finished, share your problems and solutions with the class.

Problems and Solutions in Preparing My Résumé

Problems	Solutions
English is not very good; experience in job what I want to get; explaination some technical skills.	will

Do's and Don'ts of Résumé Writing

The following is a list of the *Do's and Don'ts* for preparing a résumé, but it is mixed up. Read the list with a partner and guess which items belong with the *Do's* and which belong with the *Don'ts*. Check the appropriate box for each item.

Tips	Do	Don't
Include your Social Security number		✓
Give your date of birth	✓	
Include your mailing and e-mail addresses	✓	
Write a long, detailed résumé		✓
Write in short phrases without personal pronouns	✓	
Explain if you are married or single		✓
Include a career goal	✓	
Worry about every single word being spelled correctly	✓	
Include personal skills	✓	
Only include experience in this country		✓
Be honest	✓	
Exaggerate your job history: no one will check		✓
Write down how much you earned		✓
Explain why you need a job		✓
Include a personal goal	✓	✓

Expanding the Topic

Connecting Reading with Writing

1. Complete the résumé worksheet that follows with your own information. Then discuss your worksheet with your group. What questions do they have? Do they think it has enough information? Should you do an experience-based or skills-based résumé?

2. Use your worksheet to prepare your own résumé. The résumé should be typed. Show your completed résumé to your group, and talk about it.

3. Imagine you are applying for a job. Either choose one of the jobs on page 143, or find an interesting job in the help wanted section of your local newspaper. Write a letter of application for this job. Explain why you are interested in the job and why you believe you are a good candidate.

Résumé Worksheet

Personal information: _____
_____
_____
_____

Goal: _____
_____

Experience: _____

    Dates worked _____
    Company _____
    Job title _____
    Duties _____
_____
_____

    Dates worked _____
    Company _____
    Job title _____
    Duties _____
_____
_____

    Dates worked _____
    Company _____
    Job title _____
    Duties _____
_____

Skills:
(Include language skills, computer skills, etc.)

_____
_____
_____
_____
_____
_____

Education / Qualifications: _____
_____
_____
_____

References: _____

Exploring Online

Complete the activities using the Internet. If you need help with the computer, or have questions about doing an Internet search, ask your teacher or a classmate to help you.

1. There are different styles of résumé writing. Go online and search using "résumé" as the key word. Find examples of résumés, and bring them to class to talk about.

2. Most newspapers now publish in print and electronic form. See if your local newspaper has an online paper. Find the help wanted ads, and select four jobs you find interesting. Write a short paragraph about each job. Give as much information as possible.

3. Imagine you are the owner of a small but growing import-export business. You need an assistant to do general administrative duties. Since your major suppliers are Southeast Asian countries, you are hoping to find someone who speaks at least two languages from this area of the world. You intend to offer a good salary, benefits after three months, and a travel allowance. Go online to a newspaper, and search for classified ads. Find out how much it costs to place an advertisement. Write an advertisement for the person you are seeking. Be careful about the cost, but include as much detail as you think is important. Don't forget to use abbreviations. How much will this advertisement cost you if you run it for two weeks?

4. Imagine you have found a really great job that matches your skills. You have sent your résumé to the company, and they have invited you for an interview. You now want to prepare for the interview. Go online and search for frequently asked interview questions. Write down ten of these questions and your answers. Practice asking and answering the questions in a group.

Business World

Detach and retain this statement of earnings for your records

Employee: Michael J. Habbit ID # 334455	Employer: SystemsInc	Check date: March 15, 2004

Hours	Amount	Employee deduction	current	year to date
160.00	2400.00			
15.00 overtime	375.00	401K pension	120.00	360.00
Total gross:	2775.00	OASI	115.41	335.00
Employer contributions:		Medicare Ins.	22.43	66.98
401K pension:		Health Ins.	55.00	115.00
OASI		Federal Tax	215.00	645.00
Medicare Ins.		**Total Deductions**	527.84	1521.98
Health Ins.				
		Earnings	current	year to date
	120.00	Gross	2775.00	6111.56
	115.41	Deducted	527.84	1521.98
	22.43	**Net**	**2247.16**	**4589.58**
	225.00			

		Sick Leave as of 03.15.04	
Earned		taken	balance
15		2 (03.11-12.02)	13
		Vacation as of 03.15.04	
2		0 2	

In Reading 1, you will learn how to read and understand a paycheck. Reading 2 examines the connection between satisfied employees and good business. Reading 3 discusses the economic causes of child labor.

In this chapter, you will practice:

Reading Skills

➡ Understanding cause and effect relationships

Vocabulary Skills

➡ Choosing the correct definition from a dictionary

➡ Understanding business idioms

➡ Understanding and using negative prefixes

Life Skills

➡ Understanding a paycheck

➡ Making a personal budget

➡ Researching online

What's in a Paycheck?

Before You Read

Work in small groups. Discuss the following questions.

1. Have you ever received a paycheck? If you have, can you remember the first paycheck you got? How did you feel when you got it?

2. What information is included in a paycheck?

Choosing the Correct Definition from a Dictionary

A. The words in bold print are in Reading 1 on page 164. Read the following sentences to figure out the general meaning of the word. Then read the dictionary definitions. Write the correct definition number.

1. After Roberto paid all of his bills last month, his bank **balance** was $165.00.

> **bal·ance** /'bælens/ *n* **1** [singular, U] a state in which your weight is evenly spread so that you are steady and not likely to fall: *Billy was walking on top of the fence and **lost his balance**.* (=was unable to stay steady) | *Tricia could not **keep her balance*** (=could not stay steady), *and fell on the ice.* | *I was still **off balance*** (=unable to stay steady) *when he hit me again.* **2** [singular] a state in which opposite qualities or influences have or are given equal importance: *The car's designers wanted to **strike a balance between** safety and style.* (=make sure that two things have equal importance) **3** the amount of something that remains after some has been used or spent: *a bank balance* (=the money you have left in the bank) **4 be/hang in the balance** to be in a situation where the result of something could be good or bad: *With the war still going, thousands of people's lives hang in the balance.*

Definition number: _____

2. Juan's **gross** salary was $2,400 a month.

> **gross** *adj* **1** SPOKEN very unpleasant to look at or think about: *There was a really gross part in the movie.* | *"Yesterday, the dog threw up on the rug." "Oh, gross."* **2** a gross amount of money is the total amount before any tax or costs have been taken away: *gross income/sales*–compare NET **3** a gross weight is the total weight of something, including its wrapping **4** wrong and unacceptable: *gross inequalities in pay*–**grossly** *adv*

Definition number: _____

3. Each month Juan's expenses **come to** $1,200.

> **come to** *phr v* **1 come to do** *sth* to begin to think or feel a particular way after knowing someone or doing something a long time: *Gabby was coming to hate all the rules at camp.* **2 come to** *sb* if an idea or memory comes to you, you suddenly realize or remember it: *Later that afternoon, the answer came to him.* **3 come to $20/$3 etc.** to add up to a total of $20, $3.00 etc: *"That comes to $24.67, ma'am."* **4 when it comes to** *sth* relating to a particular subject: *When it comes to fixing computers, I know nothing.* **5** to become conscious again after having been unconscious

Definition number: _____

4. Juan wanted to buy a house, but he didn't have enough money for the **deposit.**

> **deposit** *n* **1** part of the price of a house, car, that you pay first so that it will not be sold or given to anyone else: *We put down a deposit on the house yesterday.* **2** an amount of money that is added to someone's bank account: *I'd like to make a deposit please.* **3** an amount or layer of a substance in a particular place: *rich deposits of gold in the hills.*

Definition number: _____

B. Read the following words. Scan the reading on page 164 to get a general idea of their meanings. Then look up these words in an English dictionary. Choose the definition that matches the word as it is used in Reading 1. Write the definition on the line.

Word	Definition
contribution	_____
	_____
current	_____
	_____
debt	_____
	_____
expenses	_____
	_____
net	_____
	_____
record	_____
	_____
deduction	_____
	_____
utilities	_____
	_____

What's in a Paycheck?

Michael J. Habbit is a twenty-six-year-old computer systems analyst. He has a degree in Business Management and has been working at SystemsInc for three years. He has just been promoted, and the company has given him a raise. He's decided that he wants to buy a house, because he can now afford the monthly mortgage payments. But he's worried about his finances because he has almost no savings, and therefore, nothing for a deposit. So Michael decides to review his personal finances to see what his monthly balance comes to after expenses. He wants to begin to save on a regular basis.

He begins by looking at his latest paycheck statement.

Detach and retain this statement of earnings for your record

Employee:	Employer:	Check date:
Michael J. Habbit	SystemsInc	March 15, 2004
ID # 334455		

Hours		Amount
160.00		2400.00
15.00 overtime		375.00
Total gross:		2775.00

Employer contributions:
401K pension
OASI
Medicare Ins.
Health Ins.

		120.00
		115.41
		22.43
		225.00

Earned	
15	
2	

Employee deduction

	current	year to date
401K pension	120.00	360.00
OASI	115.41	335.00
Medicare Ins.	22.43	66.98
Health Ins.	55.00	115.00
Federal Tax	215.00	645.00
Total Deductions	527.84	1521.98

Earnings	current	year to date
Gross	2775.00	6111.56
Deducted	527.84	1521.98
Net	**2247.16**	**4589.58**

Sick Leave as of 03.15.04

taken	balance
2 (03.11-12.02)	13

Vacation as of 03.15.04

| 0 | 2 |

Next Michael makes some notes about his personal budget. He writes down all of his expenses.

Monthly Expenses

apartment rent	$720.00
utilities (electric, gas, water)	$ 65.00
car payment	$200.00
gas	$ 30.00
gym—$10 a week	$ 40.00
movies, restaurants	$300.00
groceries	$200.00
clothes	$ 75.00
credit card debt of $1,156.00	
minimum payment	$165.00

After You Read

How Well Did You Read?

Work in small groups. Read the following statements. Write *T* (true), *F* (false), or *N* (not enough information). Underline the information in the reading that supports your answer.

NEI 1. Michael earns enough to make the monthly payments on a mortgage, but he doesn't have any money saved for the deposit.

_F_ 2. Michael has never missed work because of illness.

_T_ 3. Michael enjoys working out at the gym.

_F_ 4. Michael's biggest monthly expense is his car payment.

NEI 5. Michael bought a computer on credit.

Check Your Understanding

Answer the following questions in complete sentences. Pay attention to the verb tenses.

1. How much was Michael paid on March 15 after taxes and deductions were taken out of his paycheck?

   On May 15, Michael was paid $2,247.16 after taxes and deductions were taken out of his paych

2. How much has he been paid so far this year after taxes and deductions?

   So far this year, Michael has been paid $4,589.3

3. Explain the difference between gross and net pay.

   The after taxes and deductions is the difference between the total payment and the amount of taxes and deductions taken from the total

4. What benefits does SystemsInc provide for Michael?

   Systems Inc. provides Michael with health Ins. and a pensyn plan (401k) OASI, vacation time and sick days

5. How much does Michael contribute every month toward the total cost of health insurance?

   Michael contributes $55 per month for his H. In.

6. How much federal income tax has Michael paid this year?

   Michael has paid $645.00 federal income tax for this year.

7. Do you think the net amount of this month's paycheck was the same as last month's? Explain your answer.

   No, Because I don't now how many hours he worked

8. Michael would like to take a week's vacation to visit his parents. If he accrues, or earns, one vacation day per month, when will he be able to take his vacation?

   If he accrues one vacation day per month, Michael will be able to take his vacation in June.

Making a Personal Budget

There is a lot of information on the Internet about personal finances. Much of this information is published by financial companies and is free to Web users. Many people use a planning sheet to begin to organize their personal budget. Planning sheets are easy to complete and clearly show the difference between your personal expenses and income. You can search online for "personal financial planning" to find a planning sheet.

Work with a partner.

1. Look at the personal planning guide below. Using the information from Michael's notes on page 164, complete the guide. What are his net monthly savings? How much do you think he can save every month?

   _____

2. If the average new home costs $200,000, and buyers need to put down 10% as a deposit, how much does Michael need to save? Using your amount from question 1, above, how long will it take Michael to save the deposit?

   _____

3. Michael wants to reduce his monthly expenses. What item or items could he spend less on each month?

   _____

Personal Planning Guide	
Current monthly expenses:	Amount
Housing:	_____
Utilities:	_____
Transportation:	_____
Food:	_____
Activities/recreation:	_____
Clothes:	_____
Total monthly expenses:	_____
Total monthly income:	_____
Net savings per month:	_____

Happy Employees = Good Business

Before You Read

What is a good job? What makes employees happy? Read the following list of job benefits. Which benefit do you think is the most important? Rank the benefits from 1 to 10 (1 = most important). When you have finished, compare your list with a partner's and explain your choices.

Good boss	8
Good working conditions	5
Good salary	1
Good medical and dental benefits	2
Good opportunities for promotion	3
Flexible hours	9
Close to home	10
Nice coworkers	6
Professional development	7
Interesting work	4

Now Read

Read this article to find out what the writer thinks employees want from a job. As you read, pay attention to the words in bold print. If you don't understand the word, and you can't guess the meaning, look it up in an English dictionary. Choose the definition carefully. Note the definition in the margin next to the word.

Happy Employees = Good Business

1   There is a clear rule in business: High employee **turnover** is expensive. Whether you are talking about a fast-food factory with minimum wage workers or highly skilled professional employees, losing workers to another company costs companies a lot of money. First, there is the cost of **recruitment** in hiring **replacements.** Second, there is the **loss** of productivity while the business is understaffed. Third, training new employees is expensive. Successful businesses know that it is very important to encourage employees to stay with the company. Keeping employees happy makes good business sense. The question is: What makes employees happy?

2   Of course, salary and benefits are important. However, many companies today offer similar salary and benefits, so other aspects of work attract and keep good employees. Many employees report that teamwork is an essential **ingredient** for a job. While most companies maintain a structured system with supervisors, managers, directors, and a CEO, it is important that employees have a voice within the system. People want to be part of a team where they can share ideas and concerns. They want to participate in setting goals and making decisions in day-to-day management. They don't want hard-nosed supervisors and managers who won't recognize good ideas. One example of a company that encourages a teamwork style of management is Saturn, an automobile manufacturing company. According to the Saturn Web site, "There are no supervisors or time clocks, no 'us' and 'them.' There is only the shared responsibility of getting the job done right."

3   Another area of employee satisfaction is professional development and training. People want to continue to learn, and with technology changing so rapidly, companies need employees with the latest skills. Successful companies retrain current employees. Retraining improves employee **morale** and increases **retention.** Successful companies therefore encourage an **atmosphere** of learning by providing training opportunities, sending employees to conferences, and being open to sharing ideas and information.

4   When both parents work, they require help in balancing the needs of work and family life. Good companies realize this. Employees with dependable child care, generous sick leave, and good medical benefits are less likely to miss work or to leave the company. For many parents, onsite child care is a real **plus.** It saves time and usually money for the parents, who can focus more closely on their job

continued

knowing their children are nearby. Flexible hours and job-sharing opportunities also go a long way to help parents manage work and family life. These **options** make it possible for parents to make appointments with doctors, dentists, and teachers without missing time at work. There is no doubt that helping families is the right thing to do, but there is also no doubt that it makes good business sense.

5   Finally, people want to enjoy their work. They want friendly co-workers and good supervisors. They want to have a good time at work—even if the work is hard. Many people spend more hours with their co-workers than their families, so it's important that they work in a friendly environment.

6   Employees are a company's most valuable **resource.** Successful companies recognize this and offer team-based management, continual professional development, support for families to balance work and family life, and an enjoyable working environment. These thriving companies know that keeping their employees happy is an essential part of their success.

After You Read

How Well Did You Read?

Read the statements. Write *T* (true) or *F* (false). Underline the information in the reading that supports your answers.

_____ **1.** The amount of money people earn is not very important.

_____ **2.** People usually like to be part of a team.

_____ **3.** Companies that help employees meet their family responsibilities are more likely to keep employees.

_____ **4.** It costs a lot of money to hire and train new employees.

_____ **5.** A company should always hire new people when new skills are needed because retraining hurts morale.

Check Your Understanding

A. Work in small groups. Discuss the questions, and then share your ideas with the class.

1. What makes employees happy according to this writer?

2. Why do you think most people want to build their skills?

3. According to the reading, people want to play an active part in their company. They want to be able to make decisions and offer opinions. How can a manager make sure that employees have the opportunity to voice their opinions and make suggestions?

continued

B. Circle the letter of the answer that best completes each statement.

1. In the introduction, the author says that losing employees to other companies leads to _____.

   a. more accidents at work
   b. higher productivity
   c. increased business costs

2. The writer suggests that salaries and benefits are sometimes less important for companies because _____.

   a. people don't worry about money; they think more about working conditions
   b. employees value teamwork over money
   c. companies offer very similar salaries and benefits, so employees choose a company for other reasons

3. A company that has a collaborative or team-based management style _____.

   a. has no supervisors
   b. encourages all employees to work together on problem solving
   c. has a large number of directors and CEOs

4. Read this sentence from paragraph 2.

   While most companies maintain a structured system with supervisors, managers, directors, and a CEO, it is important that employees have a voice within the system.

   This sentence contains _____.

   a. a fact
   b. an opinion
   c. a fact and an opinion

5. The main idea for paragraph 3 is that _____.

   a. training employees saves the company money
   b. people want to learn new skills
   c. there are several advantages to providing professional development opportunities

6. The following statement is correct according to Reading 2: _____.

   a. Retraining leads to employees finding better jobs at other companies
   b. Retraining results in employees staying with the company for a long time
   c. Retraining is more expensive than hiring new employees

7. Onsite child care, flexible hours, and job sharing are examples of support services that can _____.

   a. decrease productivity
   b. decrease employee turnover
   c. decrease employee morale

8. The main idea of this article is that _____.

   a. supporting employees in a variety of ways is cost-effective for a business
   b. employers should understand what makes employees happy
   c. being fair to employees is the right thing to do

9. You might find this article in _____.

   a. a daily newspaper
   b. a magazine for managers
   c. a magazine for automobile employees

10. The writer tries to persuade the reader to agree with her by _____.

   a. arguing that, in her opinion, being more supportive of employees is the right way to act
   b. explaining why a more supportive business environment is advantageous to a company
   c. explaining in detail how to make employees happy at work

Choosing the Correct Word Form

A. Work with a partner. Read the words out loud. Underline the verbs you don't understand and use an English–English dictionary to find the meaning.

	Verb	Noun	Adjective	Adverb
1.	agree	agreement	agreeable	agreeably
2.	compete	competition	competitive	competitively
3.	clarify	clarity	clear	clearly
4.	complete	completion	completed	completely
5.	diversify	diversification	diverse	diversely
6.	doubt	doubt	doubtful	doubtfully
7.	energize	energy	energetic	energetically
8.	socialize	society	sociable	socially
9.	create	creation	creative	creatively
10.	attract	attraction	attractive	attractively

B. **Choose the correct word forms to complete the sentences. When you use a verb, use the correct tense and make the verb agree with its subject. The number in the chart corresponds to the item number below.**

1. It was difficult for the workers and management to _____*agree*_____ because each side believed it was right. However, after a lot of discussion, they finally signed an _____*agreement*_____.

2. Companies like Adidas and Nike _____*compete*_____ for the same customers: young people who like to wear fashionable and well-made athletic shoes. To attract these customers and beat their _____*competition*_____, each company spends a lot of money on advertising.

3. It is important to set _____*clear*_____ goals when you are helping children learn to save money. If they _____*clearly*_____ understand why they are saving, they will happily put aside the money.

4. "You must _____*complete*_____ this report by 5:00 P.M. If it isn't _____*completely*_____ finished by this time, we'll lose the sale."

5. When you plan your retirement, you should _____*diversify*_____ your savings. Financial advisers usually recommend opening a number of _____*diverse*_____ accounts.

6. The supervisor looked at me _____*doubtfully*_____ when I told him I wanted a promotion. I knew at once that I had to get rid of his _____*doubts*_____. I had to convince him I was ready for more responsibility.

7. The new boss was full of new ideas and _____*energy*_____. In fact, he was so lively, he _____*energized*_____ all of us! It was fun working with him.

8. When I first came to this country, I was surprised that my supervisor was so _____*sociable*_____. She likes to _____*socialize*_____ with everyone in the office, and she often arranges get-togethers. This was strange to me at first because in my former country, the supervisor never spoke to me.

9. Employers like people who think _____*creatively*_____. I got my current job because in my résumé, I showed how I could solve problems in a very _____*creative*_____ way.

10. The new shopping mall was very _____*attractive*_____. The bright colors and variety of stores _____*attracted*_____ a huge crowd of people on opening day.

C. Complete the following sentences using your own words.

1. His supervisor agreed to _take day off_ do her best.

2. My boss is very competitive, and she is always trying to _be on top_.

3. Could you please clarify this question because I don't _understand it_.

4. Carlos completed the application and _signed it_.

5. The company used to sell only one product, but then it diversified. Now, _they are selling a lot of products_.

6. There is no doubt that retirement _is inevitable_.

7. When he offered me the job, I shook his hand energetically and said _thanks a lot. I will take the job._

8. Because I'm not a sociable person, I sometimes feel _left out_ lonly.

9. I am a very creative person and I enjoy _the life_

10. I attracted a lot of attention at work when I _was working for software company_

inevitable — неизбежность

Understanding Business Idioms

An idiom is a group of words that have a special meaning. This meaning is different from the usual meaning of the individual words. Here are some common business idioms.

Idiom	Meaning
back to the drawing board	back to start something from the beginning
to cave in	to be forced to agree to something
to cook the books	to falsify accounts in a business
down to the wire	to be short of time
fat cat	very successful businessperson
golden handshake	a very generous retirement package
hard-nosed	very stubborn and strict
to make a killing	to make a lot of money on a deal
to have money to burn	to have so much money that it doesn't matter if you waste it
money grows on trees	the belief that money is easy to get and that you don't need to work for it

Complete the sentences using an appropriate idiom from the skill box. When you use a verb, use the correct form.

1. The owner of the business refused to pay overtime, but he _____ caved in _____ when his workers threatened to strike.

2. After winning the lottery, my brother certainly _____ had money to burn _____. He now owns three cars and is thinking of buying a fourth! What a waste.

3. The engineers worked for three years to develop a solar-powered car, but each time it failed. In the end, they decided to go _____ back to the drawing board _____ to find a completely new design.

4. Some people wonder if the _____ fat cats _____ of industry really understand how hard the average person works in his or her job. Can someone who earns millions really understand someone who earns minimum wage?

5. When the manager of the company retired, he was given a _____ golden handshake _____, which included a bonus of $50,000.

6. "Listen, people. We're getting _____ down to the wire _____. We only have two more hours to find a solution to this problem or we lose the business. Think fast."

7. I think I spoiled my children. Even though they are older, they still believe that _____ money grows on trees _____. If they need anything, my son just uses his credit card without thinking how he will pay for it; and my daughter simply smiles at her dad and says, "Please?" We should have taught them the value of money.

8. I opened the newspaper, and there was a picture of my accountant on the front page. The headline said he had _____ cooked the books _____ and was now going to jail! I couldn't believe it!

9. The manager of the shipping company was so _____ hard-nosed _____ that he refused to listen to his advisers. He always thought he knew best, and he would never change his mind.

10. In the 1990s, many people _____ made a killing _____ by buying stocks when they were low and selling them when they were high. However, many of the same people later lost money when the stock market fell in 2000.

Before You Read

Using Previewing Strategies

A. Work with a partner. Look at the photo above and read the title of Reading 3 on pages 178 to 180. Tell you partner what you think Reading 3 is about.

B. What kinds of products do you think are made by children throughout the world? Make a list of these products.

1. _____

2. _____

3. _____

4. _____

5. _____

Using Context Clues to Understand Vocabulary

H/W

Read the sentences. The words in bold print appear in Reading 3. Underline the word or words in the second sentence that have similar meanings to the word(s) in bold print. Write the meaning in your own words.

1. Children living in poverty often have an **inadequate** diet. They do not have enough nutritious food to help them become strong and healthy.

   inadequate: _They do not have enough fruit vegetable_

2. Because of the excellent weather conditions, farmers predict a very good **crop** this year. There will be plenty of agricultural products, such as corn, wheat, apples, and oranges.

   crop: _that is produced in a single season_

3. Many young people move from their villages to **urban** areas to look for employment. However, when they arrive in the cities, they find that it is very difficult to find work.

   urban: _it is areas besid city_

4. Some organizations want **consumers** to stop buying products from these companies. If people stop buying the products, these companies will change their ways.

   consumers: _people who buy from companies_

5. It is more difficult for children in **rural** areas of Peru to attend school than children in urban areas. There are fewer schools in the countryside.

   rural: _country areas_

6. In the United States **agricultural workers** are some of the poorest working people in the country. Not only are they underpaid, but many farm workers also have to move from one area to another to find work.

   agricultural workers: _farm people who works on the fields_

7. When Ali started his own business, he knew there would be no **profits** for the first month or two. Life was hard during this time, but after three months, he finally made a small amount of money.

   profits: _it is what we have after expenses in the business_

8. The organizations want people to stop buying products from companies that employ child workers. They organize **boycotts** against specific companies.

   boycotts: _to refused something_

continued

9. The Indian government is trying to **put pressure on** employers who hire child workers. They are trying to force these businesses to stop this practice.

   put pressure on: _____

10. Organizations like the International Labour Organization are trying to **abolish** the worst forms of child labor. They hope to stop these practices forever.

   abolish: _____ to officially end a law, system

Now Read

Profit at a Price

1   The term *child labor* does not refer to all children who work. It refers to children who are working long hours and doing dangerous work. These children are usually five to fourteen years old. They work in both rural and industrial areas. In agricultural areas, children as young as five years old pick crops such as apples, rice, and cocoa beans. In more urban areas, children make products like bricks, soccer balls, clothes, carpets, batteries, matches, cigarettes, and shoes. When people buy these products, they have no idea children made them. Organizations that look after children's rights believe, however, that the public should know more about child labor.

2   First of all, how many children are working as child laborers? Child labor occurs mainly in developing countries, but it is difficult to get accurate numbers of how many children are involved. International organizations estimate that 250 million children between the ages of five and fourteen are working, and that 90% of these live in Africa and Asia. India has the largest number of child workers—an estimated forty-four million, according to the International Labour Organization (ILO). The ILO monitors child labor issues around the world. Other countries also have huge numbers of child workers. Children ten to fourteen years of age make up 10% of Pakistan's workforce. There are four million child workers in the Philippines and twelve million in Nigeria. An additional seven million children are working in Brazil.

3   There are many reasons why a child has to work. The most important reason is poverty. Poverty explains why child labor happens mainly in developing countries. Children have a significant economic value in a developing country because they can earn 50% or more of their total family income—even when they are only paid pennies for their work. Children work to feed their families and themselves. In situations of terrible poverty, where money is inadequate for survival, working is a logical decision for both parents and children. Many times, parents and children work side by side sewing, digging, picking crops, or operating machinery. In some

continued

cases, parents even give or sell their children to people who promise to provide employment and education to the child. Parents hope that this will be an opportunity for the child to get a better life. According to international organizations, this rarely happens. Instead, most of the children become·slaves.

4   One person's poverty can lead to another person's profit. Child labor is part of a global economic system of low labor costs that lead to low consumer prices, which then lead to high sales in wealthy countries. Labor costs in developing countries are cheaper than in industrialized countries because people are willing to work for less money. The ILO reports that children who work up to sixteen hours a day are only paid from $1.30 to $7.00 a week. A 2002 report from the Ivory Coast found that the average annual earnings for a cocoa worker range from $30 to $110. This is not enough for a family to live on, and the children are forced to work to survive.

5   If economic reasons are the main cause of child labor, many people argue economic solutions are needed to end this problem. They believe that economic pressure should be put on countries that practice child labor. For example, other countries could add a high tax to products coming from the country practicing child labor. Critics, however, argue that this approach would make the situation worse because it would cause even more poverty. This, in turn, would lead to more children working.

6   Some organizations have a different economic solution. They want consumers to stop buying products from companies that employ child workers. These

continued

organizations organize boycotts against specific companies. They believe that if people stop buying goods produced by these companies, the companies will change the way they do business. They hope that when companies understand bad labor practices are causing them to lose money, these companies will increase wages and improve working conditions.

7   Global Exchange, an international organization that fights child labor, suggests a third economic solution to poverty and child labor: <u>fair trade.</u> Fair trade makes sure that farmers are paid a fair price for their product—a price that will allow farmers and bean pickers to feed and educate their families. For example, the international price for cocoa is about 40 cents per pound; fair trade would pay twice as much. Critics of fair trade, however, worry that if workers are paid higher wages, the cost of their product will dramatically increase. As costs increase, critics argue, people will not buy the product. Then, critics conclude, poverty will increase because farmers will not be able to sell their products.

8   The issue of child labor is very complicated. While the global community agrees it is unacceptable for children to work in these conditions, organizations and countries do not agree about how to abolish child labor. Some even believe that as long as there are rich countries and poor countries, rich people and poor people, child labor is inevitable.

After You Read

How Well Did You Read?

Read the following statements. Write *T* (true), *F* (false), or *N* (not enough information). Underline the information in the reading that supports your answer.

_____ **1.** Child labor only occurs in industrial areas.

_____ **2.** Organizations can only estimate how many children are working in difficult conditions throughout the world.

_____ **3.** Children are paid very little and therefore cannot help their families when they work.

_____ **4.** Poor education is a very important cause of child labor.

_____ **5.** Most people agree that child labor should be stopped, but they do not agree on how to stop it.

Check Your Understanding

A. Work in small groups. Discuss the questions. When you have finished, share your answers with the class.

1. Are you surprised by the number of children working throughout the world?

2. Do you agree that poverty is the most important cause of child labor? What other causes are there that the writer did not mention?

3. Do you believe boycotting a large company is an effective way to force that company to pay higher wages?

4. What is fair trade? Do you think people would be willing to pay a higher price for a cup of coffee or a bar of chocolate if they knew the people producing the coffee or chocolate were being paid fair wages?

5. Can you think of any other solutions which are not mentioned in the article?

B. Read the statements. Circle the letter of the answer that best completes each sentence. If you need to, scan Reading 3 for the words in bold print to help you.

1. According to this writer, **child labor** refers to _____.

    a. all children who work
    b. children who work instead of going to school
    c. children who work for hours at a time in difficult conditions

2. Most of the **250 million** children aged five to fourteen who work live in _____.

    a. Africa
    b. Brazil and Asia
    c. Africa and Asia

3. *Children have a significant **economic value** in a developing country because they can earn 50% or more of their total family income—even when they are only paid pennies for their work.* (paragraph 3)

    Economic value means _____.

    a. the amount children can earn through wages
    b. the amount the family pays to raise the children
    c. the amount children pay for their education

4. *Children work to feed their families and themselves. In situations of terrible poverty, where money is inadequate for survival, working is a **logical** decision for both parents and children.* (paragraph 3)

    Logical means _____.

    a. bad
    b. reasonable
    c. good

continued

5. *Labor costs* in developing countries are cheaper than in industrialized countries because people are willing to work for less money. (paragraph 4)

Labor costs means _____.

   a. the cost of working hard
   b. the cost of paying employees
   c. the value of workers

6. Some people believe industrialized countries can put pressure on countries to stop child labor by _____.

   a. adding a high tax on products from countries that use child labor
   b. passing strict laws against child labor
   c. giving money to developing countries

7. **Critics** are people who _____.

   a. support an idea
   b. disagree with an idea
   c. believe there are no solutions

8. Some companies worry that **fair trade** will result in _____.

   a. increased sales
   b. increased profit
   c. decreased sales

Reading Skill

Understanding Cause and Effect Relationships (1)

Reading 3 argues that child labor continues to exist because of poverty. This is a **cause and effect statement.** Cause and effect refers to one event resulting in or leading to another event. It is important to recognize which event is the cause and which event is the effect. To do this:

- identify the two events that are linked.
- identify the event that happened first.

The event that happened first is the cause; the event that happened second is the effect.

     The boy's parents lost their jobs. (first event: cause)

     The boy had to get a job. (second event: effect or result)

Cause and effect sentences are often connected using *because*, which always introduces the cause.

     Because his parents lost their jobs, the boy had to get a job.

Or

     The boy had to get a job **because his parents lost their jobs.**

A. Read these sentence pairs. Each pair contains a cause and an effect. First identify which is the cause and which is the effect. Underline the cause sentence and circle the effect sentence. Next, connect the sentences using *because*.

1. (My teenage daughter is always exhausted.) My teenage daughter works at a local fast-food restaurant every night.

   My teenage daughter is always exhausted because she works at a local fast-food restaurant every night.

   Or

   Because she works at a local fast-food restaurant every night, my teenage daughter is always exhausted.

2. Peter has attended three different high schools. Peter's family has moved several times in the past two years.

   _____

   _____

3. Vitaliy couldn't speak any English when he moved to England. Vitaliy attended intensive ESL classes.

   _____

   _____

4. Yuko decided to live with her host family for a whole year. Yuko liked the family a lot.

   _____

   _____

5. Ahmed wanted to buy a new laptop. Ahmed got a job in the campus bookstore.

   _____

   _____

B. There are many cause and effect ideas in Reading 3. The following events are taken from the reading. Some of these events are causes, and some are effects. Read each pair, and identify which is the cause and which is the effect. Draw an arrow from the cause to the effect. When you have finished, compare your answers with a partner's.

cmpiuks

high labor costs ⟶ expensive products
cheap products ⟵ low labor costs
child slaves ⟵ selling children
poverty ⟶ child labor
children working ⟵ hungry families
fair trade ⟶ higher prices
high taxes ⟶ more poverty
economic pressure ⟶ boycotts

Reading Skill

Understanding Cause and Effect Relationships (2)

Using *because* is one way to show cause and effect. Another way is to use cause and effect verb phrases.

> Poverty **leads to** child labor.

> Child labor **is a result of** poverty.

Leads to introduces the effect.
Is a result of introduces the cause.

Look back at Exercise B. Remember that the arrow points to the effect. Combine the sentence pairs using *leads to* and *is a result of.* Use the correct form of the verb.

1. High labor costs lead to expensive products.

2. Cheap products are the result of low labor costs.

3. Selling children leads to child slavery

4. Poverty leads to child labor.

5. Hungry families lead to children working.

6. Fair trade leads to higher prices

7. High taxes lead to more poverty

8. Economic pressure is a result of boycotts.

Understanding and Using Negative Prefixes

In previous chapters, you learned that a suffix is a group of letters added to the end of the base word. Adding a suffix changes the part of speech and sometimes the meaning of the word. A **prefix** is a letter or group of letters that is added to the beginning of the word. Unlike a suffix, a prefix does not change the part of speech. It changes the meaning of the base word.

Prefixes are very often used to make the opposite meaning of the base word: *happy—unhappy.* There are several prefixes that create opposite or negative meanings:

unacceptable	**in**adequate	**im**moral
unbelievable	**in**considerate	**im**patient
unemployed	**in**correct	**im**practical
unfortunately	**in**expensive	**im**possible
	inexperienced	

A. Read the following sentences. Complete the sentences with words from the skills box. In some cases, more than one answer is correct.

1. Many parents living in poverty want their children to have a better life. _____*unfortunately*_____, this does not always happen.

2. Some people believe the number of child workers is falling. However, this is _____*incorrect*_____, as organizations report an increase in the number of child workers.

3. When products are made in developing countries where wages are low, labor costs are _____*inexpesive*_____. In industrialized countries, it costs much more to pay workers.

4. In South Africa, many parents become _____*unemployed*_____ because they are sick with HIV/AIDS and cannot work. Their children have to drop out of school and earn money for the family.

5. Although it is _____*impossible*_____ to accurately count the number of children working full-time in difficult conditions, international organizations closely study child labor around the world. Using the information they learn, they estimate the number of child workers.

6. Some organizations like Global Exchange find it _____*immoral*_____ that children work long hours in dangerous conditions to make products sold in rich countries. They believe child labor should be stopped.

continued

7. Many governments, including India, have strict rules against illegally hiring children. However, it is ___impractical___ to think that these laws will stop child labor because the laws are not enforced.

8. When young children begin to work, they are, of course, ___inexperienced___. Because they have not done the work before, it is easy for them to have accidents and make mistakes.

9. Even when all family members are working, food is often ___inadequate___. The family is still hungry.

10. Many people are surprised when they learn how many working children there are. It's ___unbelievable___ that this happens in the twenty-first century.

B. Now complete these sentences using your own words and ideas.

1. It is unbelievable that people _____.

2. The inexperienced teacher ___won't be confortable teaching class___

3. This test is unnecessary because I ___took it before___.

4. People who sell their children are immoral because ___it lead to child slavers___

5. The student was unemployed, but he ___had a lot of money.___

6. Unfortunately, I lost ___my watch.___

7. Because the supervisor was impatient, _____.

8. It is impossible to ___solve this problem.___

9. People with cell phones are sometimes inconsiderate because they ___talk a lot.___

10. When food is inadequate, people ___get sick faster.___

Expanding the Topic

Connecting Reading with Writing

Choose one of the writing exercises. Use vocabulary that you've learned in this chapter to make your writing clear and interesting.

1. Interview a student, a friend, or a neighbor. Find out what he or she thinks is important in a good job. Ask your partner to explain his or her thoughts. For example, if he or she says flexible schedules are important, ask why. Make notes as you interview. Using these notes, write a paragraph summarizing your partner's ideas.

2. Imagine you have worked for an electrical company for many years. You have recently become a parent for the first time. Your spouse also works full-time as a teacher. It is very difficult to balance working and being a parent. You want to change your work schedule so you can have more time at home with your child. You believe this will help both your family and the company. You tried to discuss it with your boss, but he told you to put it in writing. Write a letter that clearly explains how you would like to change the schedule, why this is necessary, and how it will benefit your family and the company.

3. Imagine you are the manager of a small company that makes computer parts. You employ twenty-five people. The owner of the company, Mr. Dasai, has told you that the company is losing money because people are not buying as many computers as they did in past years. He has told you to find ways to reduce costs. Work with a group of four people. Share ideas about possible solutions. Make notes as you talk. When you have several ideas, write a memo (business letter) to the owner that clearly states the problem and several possible solutions. Make it clear which solution you think is the best, and give your reasons.

   You can begin the memo like this:

Date:	(today's date)
To:	Mr. Dasai
Fr:	(your name)
Re:	Suggestions to reduce costs

   While discussing ways we can reduce costs, we thought of several interesting suggestions. Here are our ideas:

   1. _____
      _____
      _____

   2. _____
      _____
      _____

continued

3. _____

_____

_____

4. _____

_____

_____

5. _____

_____

_____

Exploring Online

Complete the activities using the Internet. If you need help with the computer, or have questions about doing an Internet search, ask your teacher or a classmate to help you.

1. Chapter 7 is about business. What's the state of the economy today? Go to a major business site like CNNmoney.com or Fortune.com to answer the following questions:

   a. What is the current rate for a thirty-year fixed mortgage?
   b. What is the current rate for a fifteen-year fixed mortgage?
   c. What is the current unemployment rate?
   d. What is the current inflation rate?
   e. What did the Dow Jones stock exchange close at yesterday?

2. Reading 2 is about what employees want from their jobs. What qualities do you think managers want from their employees? What makes a good employee? Do an online search to find information about this topic. Write a paragraph summary of this information. Remember to include the Web addresses for your sources.

3. Reading 3 is about international organizations that are trying to educate people about the problems of child labor. Search under "child labor," and find three of these organizations. Go to their Web sites and find out more about this issue. Write a paragraph on what you find. Include the names of the Web sites you use.

CHAPTER

8

Art and Entertainment

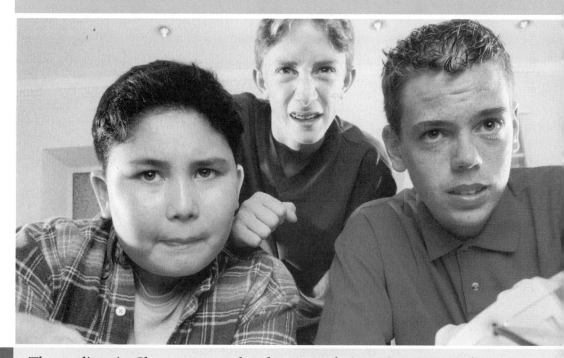

The readings in Chapter 8 are related to art and entertainment. Reading 1 is about one of the newest forms of entertainment—video games—and the effect these games might have on players. The second reading includes movie reviews for two popular movies. Reading 3 includes a short story for you to enjoy.

In this chapter, you will practice:

Reading Skills

→ Using information from other sources

→ Predicting

→ Recognizing comparisons

→ Predicting and inferring information

→ Understanding similes

Vocabulary Skills

→ Using context clues to understand vocabulary

→ Recognizing expressions

Life Skills

→ Understanding rating systems

189

Video Games: A Powerful New Kid on the Block

Before You Read

Discuss the following questions with a partner.

1. Have you ever played video games? Does anyone in your family play? What games have you played or heard of?

2. Read the title of Reading 1 on pages 191 and 192. What do you think it means? Who is the "new kid on the block"?

3. What do you think this reading is going to say about video games? Write three things you think this reading will include

   a. _____

   b. _____

   c. _____

Using Context Clues to Understand Vocabulary

The words in bold print are in Reading 1. Use context clues and circle the letter of the answer closest in meaning to the word in bold print.

1. New video games are often so popular that the demand for these games **outpaces** the supply. Customers are often disappointed that the games have already sold out.

   a. is less than
   b. is more than
   c. is the same as

2. Although the economy is not very strong at the moment, the video game industry **projects** a huge profit for the next year. People will continue to buy because they love playing video games.

   a. expects something to happen
   b. doesn't believe something will happen
   c. wants something to happen

3. There has been **rapid** growth in the sales of video games in the last few years. A few years ago, very few people played these games. Today, however, the majority of American families own and play video games.

   a. slow
   b. average
   c. extremely fast

4. Children need to learn that there are **consequences** for bad behavior. If they do something wrong, parents should discipline them. Many parents, for example, do not allow their children to watch TV if the children have behaved badly.

    a. reasons
    b. awards
    c. results

5. **Genders** are not equally represented in video games. There are more games for boys and men than girls and women.

    a. children
    b. males and females
    c. women

Now Read

Video Games: A Powerful New Kid on the Block

1.   There is no doubt that the video game industry is growing rapidly. In fact, according to a leading investment company, Bear Stearns, "growth in the game software market is likely to outpace that of the Internet (advertising), television, radio, motion pictures, music, and newspapers." In 2002, sales of video games in the United States grew by 8% and earned revenue of $6.9 billion. A further 10% growth was projected for 2003. Sixty percent of all Americans play video or computer games, and they are equally popular in many other countries. Because the games are so popular with children, many parents are now asking questions about the effects these games are having on their children. There have been several studies to try to answer these questions, but researchers have no clear answers.

2.   Researchers have found that many video games are extremely violent. A children's organization, Children Now, studied the seventy top-selling games in 2001. They found that 89% of these games were violent and almost half the games were seriously violent. For example, the top-selling game for 2001 was Grand Theft Auto. In this game, players are given stars for killing people, including police officers. The violence is senseless, and there are no consequences for killing or beating up people. This game is rated M for mature players, but it is easily available for children to play. Children Now found that even E-rated games, which are rated for everyone, contain some violence.

continued

3   Researchers also discovered that video games encourage gender stereotypes.[1] There are many more male characters than females, and many of the male characters are muscular, very strong, and aggressive. In the early video games, female characters were portrayed as helpless females who needed to be "saved" by the men. More recent video games use stronger female characters. These characters, however, often have supermodel figures and wear very revealing clothing. Therefore, one stereotype has replaced another. It is not surprising to learn that video games are designed mainly by men, for boys. It is also not surprising that girls tend to prefer computer games that have more lifelike characters.

4   It is difficult to evaluate the effect of video games on children. In *Fair Play? Violence, Gender and Race in Video Games,* Children Now reports, "Preliminary research has shown that playing violent video games can increase children's aggressive behavior and can result in emotional responses of anger and hostility. . . . Some researchers believe that compared to other visual media, the interactive nature of the games could actually increase the likelihood of aggressive behavior." However, the Interactive Digital Software Association, an organization that represents the video and computer game industry, argues that there is no proof that playing games leads to violence. They believe that youth violence is a result of other problems in society. They point out, in fact, that youth violence actually decreased in the years when video games became so popular.

5   While studies do not provide a clear answer to the question of what effects video games may have on children, there are two commonsense solutions for worried parents. First, games are rated just like movies. Parents should pay careful attention to this rating system. Younger children should only play games that are rated E—suitable for everyone. Second, anyone who has played video games knows they are addictive: You can't stop playing. Parents should therefore limit the time children spend playing games. Playing video games can be very entertaining, but parents need to watch their children carefully as they play with this "new kid on the block."

[1]**stereotype** an idea that many people have about a particular group of people, especially an idea that is wrong or unfair.

After You Read

How Well Did You Read?

Work in small groups. Read the following statements. Write *T* (true), *F* (false), or *N* (not enough information). Underline the information in the reading that supports your answer.

_____ 1. The video game industry has grown very quickly in a short period of time.

_____ 2. According to the article, girls prefer computer games that have lifelike characters.

_____ 3. Researchers have found strong proof that watching violent games leads to violent behavior.

_____ 4. The rating system used by video games is accurate.

_____ 5. Parents are questioning the effects of video games on children.

Check Your Understanding

A. Work in small groups. Discuss the following questions.

1. According to Reading 1, many video games are very violent. Do you agree with this? Why or why not?

2. What are the effects of playing violent games according to Children Now?

3. What are the effects of playing violent games according to the Interactive Digital Software Association (IDSA)? Why do you think IDSA and Children Now have different opinions about violent video games?

4. What suggestions does the reading have for parents who are concerned about their children playing video games? Do you have any other suggestions?

5. This reading focuses on the negative effects of playing video games. However, there are positive effects as well. What do you think some of these positive effects might be?

B. Read each question and circle the letter of the best answer.

1. What is the main idea of the reading?

   a. Video games are a leading form of entertainment.
   b. Video games are violent.
   c. The effects of playing video games are not clear.

2. What did Children Now find out about the seventy top-selling games in 2001?

   a. The majority of games contained violence.
   b. More than 50% of the games contained serious violence.
   c. In all games, players lost points for "killing" people.

continued

3. Which of the statements contains an opinion?

    a. Players win stars for killing people, including police officers.
    b. The violence is senseless.
    c. Grand Theft Auto was the top-selling game in 2001.

4. Read this sentence from paragraph 2.

    This game is rated M for mature players, but it is easily available for children to play.

    In this context, what does **mature** mean?

    a. experienced
    b. adult
    c. smart

5. Which of the following are examples of gender stereotypes in video games?

    a. strong, muscular male characters
    b. independent female characters
    c. male characters who need help

6. According to paragraph 3, why do girls prefer computer games?

    a. There is less violence.
    b. Female characters look more like the girls who play the games.
    c. The male characters are strong and muscular.

7. What does IDSA state about youth violence in paragraph 4?

    a. Violence in children has fallen as videos games have become more popular.
    b. Youth violence has increased in the past several years.
    c. Youth violence decreased before video games became popular.

8. What does Children Now say about youth violence?

    a. Video games are a result of violence in children.
    b. Video games can lead to aggressive behavior in children.
    c. Children are not affected by video games.

9. What statement would IDSA agree with?

    a. Children become violent when they play violent video games.
    b. Children are violent because of other problems in their environments.
    c. Children do not behave aggressively unless there is a good reason.

10. Which statement is correct?

    a. Children Now would disagree with the final paragraph.
    b. IDSA would disagree with the last paragraph.
    c. Children Now would agree with the final paragraph.

Using Information from Other Sources

When writers use information from other writers, they must always say where the information comes from. Writers do this in different ways, including **direct quotations** and **indirect quotations**. **Indirect quotations** are also known as **reported speech.**

- **Direct quotations:** These are the exact words used by the original speaker or writer. The words are within quotation marks.

  Example: "Growth in the game software market is likely to outpace that of the Internet . . ."

- **Indirect quotations** or **reported speech:** This is when the writer uses information or ideas from someone else, but puts that information into his own words. Indirect quotations and reported speech are introduced by reporting verbs and phrases such as *argues, believes, thinks, points out, states, explains, according to.*

  Example: IDSA **argues** that there is no proof that playing games leads to violence.

Work with a partner. Scan Reading 1 on pages 191 and 192 to find the answers to the following questions.

1. Where does the information come from in paragraph 1? Is this information given in direct or indirect quotations?

2. Where does the information come from in the second paragraph? How does this information support the main idea of paragraph 2?

3. What reporting verbs are used in paragraph 4?

4. Circle the direct quotation in paragraph 4. Where does this information come from?

5. Underline the indirect quotation in paragraph 4. How could you find out more information about this quotation?

Harry Potter and The Lord of the Rings

Before You Read

Work in small groups. Discuss these questions.

1. What kind of movies do you enjoy watching? Action movies? Romantic comedies? Horror movies?

2. What was the last really good movie you saw at the theater? What was it about, and why was it so good?

3. Make a list of movies your group would recommend to other students. Explain why you think other people would enjoy each movie. When you have finished, share your answers with the class.

In a movie review, a movie critic writes a short summary of the story and gives his or her opinion about the movie. Critics often award stars to show how good a movie is. Five stars means excellent; one, or even no stars, means you're better off staying at home! Look at the title of Reading 2 on pages 198 and 199. How many stars do you think these two movies will get?

Using Context Clues to Understand Vocabulary

Read the sentence pairs. The words in bold print in the first sentence are in Reading 2. Underline the word or words in the second sentence that are similar in meaning to those in bold print

1. Last week I saw a really **depressing** movie about a young girl who went to the city to find work, but ended up homeless because no one would employ her. It made me feel sad.

   depressing: _____

2. In the movie *Gandhi*, Ben Kingsley **portrays** Mohandas Gandhi brilliantly. He looks, speaks, and moves just like him.

   portrays: _____

3. Harry Potter **fans** waited for hours until the fourth book in the series was released. People who admire these books even waited in the pouring rain for their copy.

   fans: _____

4. **Special effects** are created using computer technology. Sometimes what you see on the screen looks so real you forget it is a computer-generated image.

   special effects: _____

5. The battle scene in the movie *The Patriot* was very **convincing.** At one point, the action was so lifelike I jumped out from my seat to avoid a sword-waving soldier.

   convincing: _____

Harry Potter and the Sorcerer's Stone and
The Lord of the Rings: The Fellowship of the Ring

1   Last weekend was cold, wet, and miserable, even depressing. I decided to make the best of this gloomy weather by watching two of my favorite movies from my collection. These movies chased the clouds away and turned the gray rain into dazzling sunlight. My sixteen-year-old son agreed after watching the movies with me, "They are brilliant, Dad!" I guarantee you will think so, too. *Harry Potter and the Sorcerer's Stone* and *Lord of the Rings: The Fellowship of the Ring* will go down in history as two of the best movies from the first decade of the twenty-first century. It's worth seeing them for a second time.

2   The movies share striking similarities. First of all, both come from extremely popular novels which have sold millions of copies worldwide. Devoted fans of these books looked forward to the movie versions with some nervousness. Would the movies be as good as the books? Would the actors portray the characters as magically as they are portrayed in the written print? As a fan of J. K. Rowling's Harry Potter books, and having grown up reading J. R. R. Tolkein's *The Lord of the Rings*, my answer is a resounding yes! The movies were as good as the books.

3   The movies also have similar themes: the battle of good against evil, the power of friendship, and the power of individual courage. Harry Potter is an orphan who is living with his mean aunt and uncle. On his eleventh birthday, he finds out what his relatives have known all along: He is a wizard, and a very special one at that. With the help of a giant named Hagrid, Harry travels to Hogwarts School of Witchcraft and Wizardry, where he meets two friends, Hermione and Ron. There he fights the evil Voldemort, who is trying to regain power. Likewise, in *The Lord of the Rings*, young Frodo, accompanied by friends Sam and Aragorn, must return a magical ring before it is stolen by the evil Saruman. The twists and turns of these tales will keep you guessing—even if you have read the books!

4   The special effects in both movies are masterful. In the Quidditch scene, Harry seems to soar through the theater right at the audience. Similarly, the scene where the three friends battle with "real" chess pieces will have you gripping the edge of your seat. In *The Lord of the Rings*, the special effects are perhaps even more amazing. Huge armies of terrifying monsters thunder across the screen, leaving you to wonder how on earth Frodo is going to succeed. These movies can easily stand side by side with *Star Wars* and *Jurassic Park* in terms of special effects.

5   The final similarity is the quality of acting. Chris Columbus, director of *Harry Potter*, and Peter Jackson, director of *Lord of the Rings*, chose a combination of

continued

brilliant, well-known actors and new faces. Richard Harris plays Professor Dumbledore in *Harry Potter* as masterfully as Sir Ian McKellen portrays Gandalf. Maggie Smith is amazing as Professor McGonagall in *Harry Potter*, and Cate Blanchett is a magical Galadriel. A new actor, Daniel Radcliffe, is a convincing Harry, although perhaps he is a little overshadowed by the remarkable performance of another new face—Rupert Grint as Ron. In *Lord of the Rings*, the little-known Elijah Wood plays Frodo in a charming and innocent way which makes his bravery all the more remarkable.

6   Good books live forever; good movies live almost as long. Viewers will enjoy these movies over and over again. I'm almost looking forward to the next spell of depressing weather when I will sit down and watch two more memorable movies. Meanwhile, to *Harry Potter* and *Lord of the Rings*, I award the following:

Harry Potter and the Sorcerer's Stone * * * * ½

Lord of the Rings: The Fellowship of the Ring * * * * *

Both movies are rated PG-13. Go see them. You won't be disappointed.

After You Read

How Well Did You Read?

Work in small groups. Read the statements. Write *T* (true), *F* (false), or *N* (not enough information). Underline the information from the reading that supports your answer.

_____ 1. The author thinks both are excellent movies.

_____ 2. Harry and Frodo are both orphans who fight against evil.

_____ 3. People who have read the books will not enjoy these movies.

_____ 4. According to the reviewer, the special effects in these movies are outdated.

_____ 5. These movies have similar themes.

Check Your Understanding

A. Work in small groups. Discuss the questions, and share your answers with the class.

1. According to Reading 2, in what ways are these movies similar?

2. Do you agree that sometimes a book is better than a movie? Explain your answer.

3. The reviewer points out that both movies are about the theme of good against evil. Can you think of any other books or movies that are also about this theme? List the titles of these books or movies:

   a. _____

   b. _____

   c. _____

B. Read each question and circle the letter of the best answer.

1. How is most of this reading organized?

   a. time order
   b. comparison
   c. contrast

2. In the first paragraph, why does the reviewer say he was depressed?

   a. The weather was bad.
   b. An old movie made him feel that way.
   c. *Harry Potter and the Sorcerer's Stone* made him sad.

3. In paragraph 1, how does the writer communicate his son's opinion of the movies?

   a. by using a direct quotation
   b. by using an indirect quotation
   c. by using both a direct quotation and an indirect quotation

4. Why were fans of the books nervous about seeing these movies?

   a. They thought the movies would be better than the books.
   b. They worried that the movies would not be as good as the books.
   c. They worried that the movies would not be made.

5. When did the critic read *The Lord of the Rings* for the first time?

   a. just before he watched the movie
   b. when he became a movie critic
   c. when he was a child

6. Who represents "good" in these two movies?

   a. Harry, Hermione, and Ron
   b. Gandalf and Voldemort
   c. Harry and Frodo

7. In paragraph 3, what does the transition *likewise* introduce?

   a. an additional example
   b. a similar example
   c. a contrasting example

8. What does the writer think of the special effects in these two movies?

   a. They are better than *Star Wars* and *Jurassic Park*.
   b. They are not as good as *Star Wars* and *Jurassic Park*.
   c. They are the same quality as *Star Wars* and *Jurassic Park*.

9. Which statement is correct according to the reading?

   a. Richard Harris is a better actor than Sir Ian McKellen.
   b. Rupert Grint gave a better performance than Daniel Radcliffe.
   c. Elijah Wood was not very convincing as Frodo.

10. Why is this critic "almost looking forward to the next spell of depressing weather"?

   a. Because he will be able to watch *Harry Potter* and *Lord of the Rings* again.
   b. Because he will have time to watch two different movies.
   c. Because he likes the rain.

Reading Skill

Recognizing Similarities

Reading 2 **compares,** or looks for similarities between, two movies. Writers use signals to introduce comparisons. These signals include:

like   both   likewise   similarly   as _____ as

Examples:

Like Frodo, Harry is a young boy who has to fight evil.

Both authors of these novels are British.

Harry is helped by two friends—Hermione and Ron. *Likewise* (or *similarly*), Frodo is helped by Sam and Aragorn.

The movies are *as* good *as* the books.

Recognizing these signals helps you to understand the reading more easily.

A. Reread the article on pages 198 and 199. Underline the words that signal comparisons.

B. Now, using the underlined words to help you, complete the following chart showing the comparisons from the reading.

	The Sorcerer's Stone	The Fellowship of the Ring
Represents good:		Frodo
Represents evil:		
Loyal, trustworthy friends:	Ron and Hermione	
Scenes with excellent special effects:		
Well-known actors:		
New, less-known actors:		
Rated:		
Authors of original books:		

Recognizing Expressions

In English, many words are often used together as a phrase or an **expression.** In order to understand an expression, you need to use context clues from the sentences around the expression. It is not helpful to translate each separate word.

For example,

> I **made the most of** this gloomy weather by previewing two movies which chased the clouds away and turned the gray rain into dazzling sunlight.

> To make the most of something: to take advantage of a situation that is not perfect.

Reading is an excellent way to build your knowledge of expressions. You should remember expressions as phrases rather than individual words.

A. The following expressions are in Reading 2. Scan the reading on pages 198 and 199 to locate them. Use context clues and match the expression with the correct definition.

_____	**1.** go down in history as	**a.** to be of equal quality
_____	**2.** twists and turns	**b.** full of excitement or fear
_____	**3.** gripping the edge of your seat	**c.** be remembered as
_____	**4.** stand side by side with	**d.** rapidly changing story

B. Now complete the sentences in your own words.

1. The Columbia shuttle disaster in 2003 will go down in history as _____

    _____.

2. There were so many twists and turns to the story that I _____

    _____.

3. I found myself gripping the edge of the seat because _____

    _____.

4. In my opinion, *Star Wars: Episode II—Attack of the Clones* cannot stand side by
    side with the first *Star Wars* movie. The first movie was _____

    _____.

Life Skill

Understanding Rating Systems

Parents want to make sure that their children are watching appropriate (suitable)
movies at the theater and on TV. They also want their children to play appropriate
video games. To help parents decide which movies or games are suitable for their
children, many countries have rating systems. Parents can look for a clear icon, or
symbol, that indicates the age suitability for the movie or the game. For example, a
film that is rated G, for general audiences, is appropriate for children of all ages.

A. Read these ratings out loud with a partner. If you don't understand a word, try to guess its meaning. If you can't guess, look it up in an English dictionary.

Movies

G   **GENERAL AUDIENCES**
All Ages Admitted

PG   **PARENTAL GUIDANCE SUGGESTED**
Some Material May Not Be Suitable For Children

PG-13   **PARENTS STRONGLY CAUTIONED**
Some Material May Be Inappropriate for Children Under 13

R   **RESTRICTED**
UNDER 17 REQUIRES ACCOMPANYING
PARENT OR ADULT GUARDIAN

NC-17   NO ONE 17 AND UNDER
ADMITTED

Video Games

eC   Content may be suitable for ages 3 and older. Contains no material that parents would find inappropriate.

E   Content suitable for ages 6 and older.

T   Content may be suitable for persons 13 and older. May contain violent content, mild or strong language, and/or suggestive themes.

M   Content may be suitable for people 17 and older. May contain mature themes or more intense violence.

A   Adults only. Not intended for persons under 18.

RP   Rating pending.

B. **Work with a partner. Answer the questions in complete sentences. When you have finished, share your answers with the class.**

1. Do you think rating systems successfully protect children from playing or seeing inappropriate games and movies? Explain your answer.

   _____

   _____

   _____

2. In your country, what happens if two fifteen-year-olds try to get into a movie intended for an adult audience?

   _____

   _____

   _____

   _____

3. Imagine that your favorite TV show is a movie. What movie rating would you give it? Explain your answer and give reasons.

   _____

   _____

   _____

   _____

Before You Read

Predicting and Inferring Information

When you read for pleasure, you do not normally preview the reading by skimming for the main ideas. You want to read carefully, understanding as much as possible. You also try to predict what is going to happen next by inferring or guessing as you read.

Fiction writers sometimes don't state information directly. It can be more interesting when the writer gives clues. Then the reader infers information and draws his or her own conclusions.

Example:

As he moved through the tables in the restaurant, Jim felt his knees weaken with every step. His hands were sweating and he was sure his face was red. A few feet from her table, Jim paused and took a deep breath. With a smile in place, he stepped forward to face her.

What can you infer about Jim? <u>He is nervous.</u>

What clues help you infer this? <u>His knees feel weak, his hands are sweating,</u>
<u>and his face is red.</u>

Read the paragraph. As you read, look for clues to help you infer information. Then answer the questions that follow.

Paragraph 1

The old man pulled his two ill-fitting coats tighter and huddled down on the park bench. His faithful dog whined briefly, and then settled in its usual spot at the old man's feet. Garbage flew around, and leaves were torn too early from the nearby trees. Petals from the last roses in a nearby flower garden fluttered like confetti around the bench. The old man pulled his knitted hat over his ears and seemed to almost disappear into the drab grays and browns of the shelter handouts. He crossed his legs for warmth, and rubbed his hands together. He closed his eyes, forgot about his hunger, and thought of better times.

1. What can you infer about this old man? _____

    What clues help you infer this? _____
    _____
    _____
    _____

2. What's the weather like? _____
    _____
    What clues help you infer this? _____
    _____
    _____

3. What time of the year is it? _____
    _____
    What clues help you infer this? _____
    _____
    _____

4. Has he always been homeless? _____
    _____
    What clues help you infer this? _____
    _____
    _____
    _____

Paragraph 2

Kelly looked at her watch for the third time in two minutes. No, she wasn't late. She smoothed her skirt and checked that her hair was still in its neat pony tail. It was very quiet in the room. She could almost hear her heart beating furiously, and she wondered if the receptionist could hear it, too. She took a deep breath. The receptionist glanced over, and smiled. A buzzer sounded. The door opened, and a man and a woman appeared. Both were smiling as they shook hands. The man left and the woman walked over to Kelly, arm outstretched. "You must be Miss Young. I'm Janet Reid. Please come in." Kelly stood up, clutching her résumé in her hand, and followed the woman in.

1. What is Kelly waiting for? _____

   What clues help you infer this? _____

   _____

2. How does she feel? _____

   What clues help you infer this? _____

   _____

   _____

3. Why does the receptionist glance at Kelly? _____

   How do you know? _____

Now Read

The first chapter in this book included a short story for you to enjoy. This last chapter ends with another short story about a man with a secret. As you read, look for clues to help you make inferences about this story.

Another Day at the Office

1   "I've made you a nice sandwich for lunch, John. Cheese and tomato—your favorite. And I put a little surprise in with it. Have a nice day, dear. Don't forget you promised you'd be home early. Bye now. Don't get too wet. Look at those clouds—a storm's coming."

2   John Watson smiled at his wife as he walked down the driveway. Rounding the corner to Main Street, he took a deep breath, squared his shoulders, and joined several other men and women walking toward the station. Like Watson, each wore a dark suit and carried a briefcase and a black umbrella. They were headed for the 7:30 express train which would deliver them at precisely 8:17 at King's Cross Station. There they would separate as each walked to the offices: lawyers, accountants, businessmen. Another work day was beginning.

continued

3   Watson reached platform 3A and took his customary seat on the wooden bench closest to the newspaper stand. There was a clap of thunder off in the distance. He nodded at the middle-aged man already sitting on the bench, newspaper in hand.

4   "Morning, James. Anything happening in the world today?"

5   "Morning, John. Nothing we can't fix at the office."

6   Watson smiled. Fifteen years and the greeting never changed. The 7:30 roared into the station.

7   As the train arrived in the city, the storm broke. Umbrellas were opening up everywhere like winter flowers reaching for the rain. Watson turned up his collar, braced himself against the cold wind, and strode purposefully toward the law firm of Elderberry, Glover, and Sons. Fifteen years.

continued

8   As he approached the familiar Victorian building with the brass plaque proudly announcing the partners' names, he felt the cold hit him in the chest. His hand holding the umbrella against the bitter cold trembled and felt as cold as ice. He staggered slightly. Then, once again, he took a deep breath and walked on past the office of Elderberry, Glover, and Sons.

9   King's Street Library opened at 9:00. Watson was there as the heavy oak doors were unlocked by the librarian. He went in, relieved to be out of the weather. The librarian smiled at him, but as he passed, she looked over to her colleague and gently shook her head. The colleague glanced at Watson, and then looked away. They knew, and he knew they knew, but no one said a word. Watson walked over to the newspaper section, took a copy of the *Times,* and silently sat down to read.

10   It was quiet in the library. The wooden floors and paneled walls kept out the noise of the city. Watson read and the clock ticked steadily. His thoughts wandered away from the black and white ink to settle on his current situation. "Unemployed," he thought. "That's what I am. I am a fifty-three-year-old, unemployed, senior office manager. And I have no idea what I'm going to do."

11   He heard the noon chimes and carefully folded the paper and replaced it on its stand. Taking his briefcase and umbrella, he quietly left, avoiding the gentle eyes of the librarian. The rain had stopped, and the city air felt unusually clean as he made his way toward the park. Another new routine. Same bench; same pigeons gathering hopefully just beyond his reach. He unwrapped his sandwich, and picked at it. The pigeons took his lack of appetite as a hopeful sign, and ventured closer. He rewarded them with a crust, and then fed them the rest of the sandwich piece by piece. He found the surprise at the bottom of his lunch bag. A slice of fruit cake. That, too, went to the birds.

12   "Tonight," he thought, "tonight I'm going to tell her. Yes. Tonight. It will be all right. I'll tell her tonight."

continued

13   He stood up, stiff from sitting in the cold. Brushing the crumbs from his neatly pressed suit, he began to walk to his afternoon refuge: the National Museum. As he left the park, a carelessly thrown newspaper fluttered in the grass like an injured bird. It came to rest beside the bench. The front page rippled slightly in the wind, and mud blurred the small print, but the headline was clear for all to see: "Unemployment at 8.5% and still rising."

14   John Watson walked out of the park. "Tonight," he told himself. "Tonight."

After You Read

How Well Did You Read?

Work with a partner. Read the statements. Write _T_ (true), _F_ (false), or _N_ (not enough information). Underline the information in the story that supports your answers.

_____ 1. John's wife believes he is going to work every day.

_____ 2. John used to have a good job.

_____ 3. John spends all day in the library instead of going to work.

_____ 4. John spends the afternoon walking around the park.

_____ 5. John is planning to tell his wife that night.

Check Your Understanding

Answer the questions in complete sentences.

1. How does John get to the city each morning?

   _____

2. How long has John known James?

   _____

3. Why does John go to the library?

   _____

4. What was John's previous job?

   _____

5. Does John enjoy the surprise his wife packed for him? Explain your answer.

   _____

continued

6. Where does John spend his afternoons?

_____

7. Are a lot of people unemployed like John? How do you know?

_____

Inferring Information

You will need to infer information in order to answer these questions. Find and reread the necessary parts of the story before you begin each answer. Answer in complete sentences.

1. How does John feel as he walks past the offices of Elderberry, Glover, and Sons?

_____

_____

2. Why do you think the sight of this office makes him feel like this?

_____

_____

3. What do the two librarians do as John enters the library? Explain why you think they do this.

_____

_____

_____

4. Why doesn't John look at the librarian as he leaves?

_____

_____

5. What is John going to tell his wife that night? Why hasn't he already told her?

_____

_____

_____

_____

Understanding Similes

Good writers choose their words very carefully in order to make the story come alive for the reader. When you read good writing, you can almost imagine you are in the story. You can see what the writer is describing. Writers use many techniques to make their writing exciting. One technique is to use **similes.** A simile is an expression that describes something by comparing it with something else, using the words *as* or *like.*

> The lake was as clear as glass.

> The rain was like a solid wall of water.

Work with a partner.

1. Scan Reading 3 on pages 208 to 211 to find four similes. Underline the similes.

2. Do the similes make the writing more real for you? Talk about this with your partner.

3. Practice writing your own similes. Complete the following sentences.

   a. The snow on the winter trees looked like _____
   _____.

   b. My teenage son was sleeping as peacefully as _____.

   c. When I heard the good news from the doctor, I felt like _____
   _____.

   d. The wind howled through the trees like _____
   _____.

   e. Her eyes are as blue as _____.

Expanding the Topic

Connecting Reading with Writing

Choose one of the following writing exercises. Use vocabulary that you've learned in this chapter to make your writing clear and interesting.

1. Using your notes from the chart you completed on page 203, write a paragraph summary of the similarities between *Harry Potter and the Sorcerer's Stone* and *The Fellowship of the Ring.* Use a variety of comparison signals. Begin your paragraph as follows:

   > According to the reviewer, there are many similarities between <u>Harry Potter and the Sorcerer's Stone</u> and <u>The Lord of the Rings: The Fellowship of the Ring</u>.

2. Do you think video and computer games are good for children? Write a paragraph that answers this question and explains your opinion.

3. Imagine you are a movie critic. Choose a movie you have seen recently and write a review about it. Use Reading 2 to help you plan your writing. Don't forget to include how many stars you award the movie and its rating.

4. The ending of the story *Another Day at the Office* is left to the reader's imagination. How do you think this story should end? Using your imagination, write the ending of this story. Begin with the following sentences:

> The sky was already dark as John walked up to his house. He briefly rested his face against the cool glass of the front door. Then, turning his key firmly in the lock, he walked in and called out . . .

Exploring Online

Complete the activities using the Internet. If you need help with the computer, or have questions about doing an Internet search, ask your teacher or a classmate to help you.

1. Imagine you are taking care of three children ages six, eight, and twelve. It's a rainy day, and you want to take them to the movies. Go online and find the nearest movie theater. Find out which movies are playing. Choose a movie that you think the children would enjoy and that would be appropriate for all the children. What time does the movie start? What is it rated?

2. Parents are also concerned about TV violence and the effect it has on children. Go online and search for information about this topic. Find one article that is short and easy enough for you to understand. Read it, and prepare a short oral presentation about TV violence and children. Remember to say where you found the information.

3. *Harry Potter and the Sorcerer's Stone* and *The Lord of the Rings: The Fellowship of the Ring* were both the first movies in a series. What movie followed *The Sorcerer's Stone*? What movie followed *The Fellowship of the Ring*? Do an online search to find out. Then find a review for each of the second movies. Did critics like the second movies as much as the first?